The Place He Made

February 17, 19

Peterborough

for Nat Ireland

with pleasure

E d i e

C l a r k

Edie Clark

The Place He Made

Villard Books New York 1995

Grateful acknowledgment is made to Another Sundown Publishing Co. for permission to reprint an excerpt from "Safe at Anchor" by Kate Wolf. Copyright © 1979 by Another Sundown Publishing Co. (BMI). Used by permission.

A shortened version of the last chapter of this work appeared in the May 1994 issue of *Yankee* magazine.

Library of Congress Cataloging-in-Publication Data
Clark, Edie (Edie Sterling)
The place he made / Edie Clark. — 1st ed.
p.   cm.
ISBN 0-679-43875-0 :
1. Clark, Edie (Edie Sterling)   2. Bolton, Paul.   3. Northfield
(N.H. : Town)—Biography.   I. Title.
CT275.C62159A3   1995
974.2'72—dc20
[B]   94-41638

Manufactured in the United States of America on acid-free paper.
24689753
First Edition

for Paul,
because this was the only thing left I could do.

Acknowledgments

For help in preparing this book and for love and support during Paul's illness and after, I send unending thanks to Nancy Hopkin; Jud Hale; Mel Allen; Andre Dubus and all the Thursday Nighters (especially Christopher Tilghman, Jim Thomson, Debra Spark, Jack Herlihy, Kathleen Cushman, and Marian Novak); George Odell; Carolyn and Michael Chute. To Aunt Peg and Uncle Jamie Odell (also for the clean sheets on Thursday nights); my parents, Dot and Lu Clark; my sister, Chris Clark, and her husband, Charlie Brooks and all the staff at Mountain Home Lodge; all the wonderful nurses on the fourteenth floor at Dana Farber Cancer Institute; Ed and Susan Hand; Genevieve Drevet; Dr. Marcia Liepman; Carol and Charley Dane; Susan Bolton; David Novak; Marie Kirn; Lary Bloom; Jamie Young; John Pierce; Steve Muskie; Sharon Walker; Laurette Carroll; Sandy Taylor; Sy Montgomery; Hazel Odell; Lindsley Hand; Mac and Marcia Odell; the phantom sheetrocker from New England Wood Designs; David Voorhis and Polly Bannister; Bryan Trudelle; Jim Collins; Reverend Herb Henry; Reverend Richard Seaver; Reverend Robert C. Harvey; Reid Harvey; Nate Harvey; Suzi and Geoffrey

Harvey; John Spencer; Betty and George Austermann; Julie Rowse, and to the memory of Dave; Lida Stinchfield; Annie Card and the folks at Tolman Pond; Ellen Sordillo; Beth Smith; Pat Donnelly; Claudia Cleary-Nichols; Rosemary James; Mary and Arthur Doyle; Michael Miller; Alexis Leino; Brice Raynor; Harvey Tolman; Reverend Mary Upton and the good people of the Combined Parish of Harrisville and Chesham; Dr. Jonathan Niloff; Dr. Richard Stein; all of the doctors at Dana Farber; Hospice of the Monadnock Region; Ron Miller; David Kennard; the generous people at Wellesley College; and all my friends at *Yankee* magazine.

In addition, gratitude to my editor David Rosenthal as well as to the keen eye of Jean-Isabel McNutt.

And special thanks to Felice Smith Fullam and the memory of her partner, Harvey Smith.

Part One

1

When I think back on Paul, the Paul I knew at the very beginning, what I remember most is his room. It was not a place I was invited to right away. In fact, I had known him at least a year before I was welcomed inside. It was a winter evening, and Paul had asked me for dinner, with him and with his father, Arthur. When I got there, Arthur had been expansive, attentive, acted almost as if I'd come to visit him rather than Paul. Paul sat quietly and then, after an hour or so, he got up and said to me, "Come. I want to show you something," and crooked his finger toward the stairway. The stairs were behind a door off the dining room, and they were as narrow and steep as a stairway can be without being a ladder. The treads were just wide enough for the balls of my feet. The bottom of the stairs was stacked high with old newspapers and magazines and cans of roofing cement. At the top of the stairs, what he called his "room" was actually a small apartment, a space that when he was growing up was divided into bedrooms for all the kids. His two sisters got the best space—because they were girls, he had once explained to me—and his brother, Donald, had a temper so he usually got what he wanted. Paul never made a fuss, so he ended up living in the attic; in the summer he pitched a tent in the backwoods and lived there. After they left, one by one, he moved down from his attic and this is where he stayed, paying rent to his mother, long after the others left, gradually absorbing their space.

This odd arrangement of tiny rooms had been untouched since the thirties, maybe earlier. There were various fixtures around the place—an old sink and an old refrigerator, but they didn't seem in use. The bathroom was the same—the fixtures very old, streaked with rust. The faded blue wallpaper was torn away in places, long dreary water stains running halfway down the walls. The plaster had fallen away in spots, leaving the ribs of the lath exposed. In fact, I remember wondering if Paul used it, or if it was just kept as a storage room. There was plenty to support that theory. In various corners and in the big old sink were piles and heaps of things, some covered with sheets, some not. This, he explained, was stuff his sister Susan had left there to be stored. Susan was the wild one, who lived in exotic places. She would send Arthur postcards and Paul would show them to me—from Provincetown or the Virgin Islands. She never stayed anywhere very long and I think at that point she was living in St. John, working as a cook on chartered sailboats. She left her clutter behind. Paul didn't seem to mind. He moved around the piles as if they were part of the structure.

Beyond the bathroom there were two other small rooms. In one he had a bed and a desk. The bed was lengthwise under the eaves, so that, I imagined, when he got into bed the roof line would pass over him close as a casket cover. The other room was more like a walk-in closet and at least half of it was stacked with more of Susan's stuff. The other half had Paul's drafting table and drawing supplies.

In many ways it was like the cabin of an eccentric old man. The windowsills were lined with tiny collectibles: old bottles, lanterns, vases, things he had found in the woods, in the walls of other people's homes or in houses he had remodeled. On the tops of tables and the desk and his file drawers was an endless assortment of oddities—tobacco tins, kettles and trivets. Both rooms were papered in ancient floral-design wallpaper, and the window curtains were ragged with age. He had the walls covered with posters, pictures of me, pictures of my dog, Gorm, pictures cut from magazines of cars and animals, topographical maps of the area. I reached up to touch one and he said, "Oh, watch out." I suppose I looked surprised, so he went on to explain, "I have to put these up to keep the plaster from coming down." Under my fingertip I could feel the dust poised behind the poster and then I could see that all these pictures did literally hold up the crumbling walls.

"Oh, Paul!" I said, and he came over and put his arms

around me and held me for a moment. Then he said, "Please don't feel sorry for me."

This is a story I never thought I would tell. It is the story of a love, the love I shared with a man who came into my life almost surreptitiously, a man who loved me in the most complete way and then died. If he had not died, I would not be telling this story. It is either the way he loved me or the way he died that compels me to write this, but I cannot divide the two.

In truth, I have been writing about him since I first knew him. When I first started writing about him, there was no story. I wrote about Paul in much the same way an artist pulls off to the side of the road to sketch a scene that has captured her. Mostly descriptive passages, in my journals and in letters to friends who lived far away. "Jeff is working with someone new," I would start out and then go on to tell of this carpenter who had come to work with my husband.

The oddness of his appearance made my attraction to him all the more confusing. A small-town, quick take on him was simply that he was strange, but most of that had to do with the way he dressed, the baggy clothes, the old-fashioned shoes and hat, the black-rimmed eyeglasses. Looking beyond that, I saw a lot else, which was even more perplexing. His face held both kindness and darkness. He had brooding brown eyes and an almost childlike face, yet one that held mystery. He was twenty-seven (a year younger than I, seven years younger than Jeff) when we first knew him, but it was hard to guess his age. He looked older, probably because of his clothes: he didn't wear the usual faded jeans and T-shirts, but green work clothes that hung loosely on him, and on his feet he wore black hard-toed shoes rather than the tan work boots most carpenters preferred. Instead of the name-brand baseball caps, he wore cloth caps, the kind old men wear. I'd never seen a young man wear hats like that. His stories were what drew me in. He had an old-fashioned way of speaking, spiced with a New Hampshire twang, and he liked to tell stories about his people, who had farmed the land where, much more recently, Jeff and I had built our house.

Beneath the baggy clothing, Paul had a wonderful strong body and I used to love to watch him work. When he did so, the oddness fell away and an enormous power and strength came forth—a mastery, I suppose.

When he first came to work with Jeff, he had no power tools, only hand tools. I can remember that Jeff thought this was incredible, as if he'd discovered an antique stashed away in an attic. But he didn't treasure it. Though he found it amusing and enjoyed telling our friends about it (in fact, I think he bragged a bit, about how Paul could put a cabinet together without ever using a single nail), overall, he thought it archaic and detrimental.

I found it amazing to watch Paul cut a board with a hand saw. He'd pump a few times and *slap,* the board would fall in two. When he used a plane, the motion seemed to come all the way from his toes to produce the new contour in the wood. Frilly piles of yellow curls would froth up as he worked. Periodically, he'd stop and brush the shavings away with his hand, a movement almost like a caress.

I wasn't at all sure power tools had anything to offer Paul. Still, Jeff began a campaign to convince him to "go power." He was successful, to some degree. Within a few months, Paul had purchased a circular saw and only used the hand saw for special cuts. He also stopped using the old folding rule in favor of the snap-back steel tapes that most carpenters attach to their belts.

The new tools didn't alter his style. He worked with wood in a gentle, respectful way and it was my first clue to his grace. It didn't matter, really, whether he was making a cabinet or working outdoors in the woods. He used to come over sometimes and work with Jeff, helping to cut cordwood when there wasn't much carpentry to be done. I'd go out and help them, hauling brush or loading the truck. But sometimes I would just stop and sit and watch. Jeff, when he split wood, reminded me of an ax murderer: he'd reel back, lift the ax above his head and with a great show of muscle smash down against the upright log. In the course of an afternoon, he'd sweat and tire easily, while with Paul it was almost like ballet. He'd lift his ax in an effortless arc and let it drop down onto the log, which would open like a flower on the forest floor.

There was a rhythm, a special touch in his work such as I've only ever seen with artists who are completely in contact with their medium. He would sometimes stop and run his finger across whatever he was working on, which suggested to me not only precision but a deep connection, an unspoken love.

Paul was not big, but he was strong in the most natural way, as if he had grown up out of the ground from a root. He seemed to span all time, and as we grew closer I saw in his eyes a kind of wisdom I could not possibly quantify, while others continued to dismiss him as an oddball; one neighbor said, on hearing Paul had come to work with Jeff, "Oh, Paul Bolton—he's a nutcase, isn't he?" Another neighbor told me he thought Paul was gay—*queer* was the word he used—but when I asked him why, his reason was that Paul lived at home and he'd never seen him with a woman. I could not name what he was, but he was neither of those. He was different, distinctly different from the rest of us.

Though he was a grown man, he lived still in his father's house, down in the next town, and did not seem to have a life outside of his work, which absorbed him, and outside of taking care of Arthur, his father, who had apparently come undone, in the silent, desperate way of an old carpenter. What had happened, several years before I knew Paul, was that his mother had left, moved out of that house, where she and Arthur had raised their four children, of whom Paul was the oldest. She was at the time probably in her fifties and she had recently earned her degree in music from Smith. She was an organist, a church organist. She had come home one day, Paul told me, and said she was moving out and then she did, Paul and Arthur loading her things, including the piano and the two organs, into the

backs of their pickup trucks, and driving them to the apartment on the quiet side street she had chosen for her new
home, her new life. No one said anything. I wasn't there,
but I know this is so. This is the way of this family.

Afterward, Paul felt responsible for Arthur. He
cooked for him and kept the wood fires burning in winter
and in summer kept the lawn mowed and grew beans and
beets and tomatoes in the garden behind the house. In the
evenings, they sat at the kitchen table and watched television wordlessly.

Paul had never been to the movies, ever, though Jeff
and I urged him to come with us. In fact, whenever we
asked Paul to do something with us after work he would
always decline, saying Arthur expected him. I asked him
once why he felt he needed to do this and he said simply,
"Because I'm the oldest."

At the time this sense of duty and loyalty to family
seemed old-fashioned to me. But then, I didn't know Paul
very well. It was a while before I realized he saw the world
through a completely different lens.

Once, very early in our friendship, we all went to a
party together. Paul and Jeff had renovated an old farmhouse and the owners, who were casual friends of Jeff's and
mine, invited all three of us to an open house to show off
the beautiful new kitchen cabinets and the fancy greenhouse. They were college professors and I knew their circle
of friends. So when Paul arrived at our house dressed in an
ill-fitting plaid jacket and an old-fashioned tie, I felt uncomfortable for him, wondering if he might not feel out of
place among all the young socialites. But at the party, while

cocktails were in full swing, I mingled sociably and then went and sat near him on the porch, a big wide front porch, open to the woods beyond the house. It was a lovely summer evening. The sun had not yet set. Sophisticated party chatter swirled all around us. We sat quietly. At last Paul said, "Did you hear that?" I wondered what snippet of conversation he was referring to.

"What?" I asked.

He waited a minute before he put up his finger and said, "There, there it is again. A cardinal." And for the first time, I heard the birds singing beyond the porch.

My life at the time we met was as dark as his, in a very different way. What moved us both was the power of love, and I never until that time had believed in anything even remotely like it. But it was not a love I recognized right away and, just like anything worthwhile, it did not happen very quickly.

It was the winter that Jeff spent in Montana that our marriage fell apart. It had never been solid, but because of the way we lived and because of where we lived, it had been hard for us to separate, though we had agreed that we should. It was the land, which I knew from the information on our deed had been the land of the Boltons since the early 1800s, that held me. I could take you now, still, to places where the woods open out into a wide field of sword-tipped ferns, a burst of light green in the forest deep. I could take you to an old maple tree, huge and gnarled, big around as any I'd ever seen, reaching way up into the sky. It was beside a small stream, and I used to like to go there—

far into the woods on a path once used by loggers—and lean back against its incredible girth and dream. I can still go to where the deer live and find the cleft in a rock face that is a bear den and I can go too to the spring, a mile back in the woods, up on a hill, whose sweet waters ran down into the kitchen sink of the old farmhouse, where we lived for several years before building our house just below.

The house we built was meant to endure what we believed was the inevitable decline of civilization. We heated it with wood we cut from the forest behind the house and I cooked on a stove that used only wood for fuel. We pumped our water by hand from a well we'd dug ourselves and we heated the water with sunlight and composted our waste inside a big fiberglass tank in the cellar. In the evenings we read by the light of kerosene lanterns and fell asleep under windows that looked up into the heavens. We raised chickens for meat and grew most of our food in the gardens that surrounded the house.

There was a terrible division here. While I loved the land and the animals and the work and the way the light crossed the hill in the afternoon, I knew I was sharing my life with a man who was capable of confusing me with his charm and absurdist sense of humor. But there was another side to Jeff. One night, during a storm that drifted snow to the windowsills, he bruised me so badly that we both knew I'd have to go to the emergency room. On the way to the hospital, he convinced me to tell them it had been a sledding accident. I could tell that the doctor there did not believe out story. I hoped he would turn Jeff in to the police, but that blew over, like the other times. This was not a constant battering but a measured distribution of his power, enough to keep me scared. I never left for a lot of reasons. For one, we had created a life that was outside the mainstream. Many of our friends and family had questioned this. To leave would be to admit defeat. And then there were the guns. Jeff had at least a dozen guns, high-powered shotguns as well as handguns. His favorite was a .357 Magnum, which he liked to clean as he sat on the edge of our bed, smoothing the barrel with the soft cloth he kept in a plastic pouch. This gun was thick and brutal, the ugliest instrument I'd ever seen. He kept these weapons under the bed. I never knew what he was going to do, and when he felt it would work, which it did, he used the guns as a threat. He was also sufficiently charming so that I thought no one would believe me if I told them about this other side. Sometimes I didn't even believe it myself. His remorse was always plentiful and convincing, his sense of humor infallible. Yet all of this left in me a lingering residue of fear.

Jeff left right after Christmas. He was going to spend four months in Montana building an addition onto the house of a friend. He packed his tools into the back of his old Volvo wagon and I took his picture, standing beside the comically overloaded car. We stood in the snow, saying good-bye. It was not meant to be a parting, but there was a sense of excitement for both of us as he left. It felt as if the great impasse in our marriage was finally moving, *something* was finally happening. We hugged and promised to write. He closed the hatch on the wagon and got into the car and started it up. "Hold down the fort," he said, putting it into gear, and then as the car began to move he leaned out his rolled-down window, looked straight at me, his green eyes turning cold, and said, "Whatever you do, don't call Paul for anything."

Of course I called him. When the ice backed up on the roof or when the tractor wouldn't start, Paul always came, and he would take care of things, making everything seem so simple. It was more than that, though. I missed Paul. Before Jeff left, I had seen Paul every day. He came up to the house early, before seven. Jeff was always late getting out of bed, but I was up, pushing sticks of wood into the cookstove, heating the water for coffee, and Paul would come in the back door. We usually had time for a cup of coffee together, talking quietly about what our day would hold, before Jeff came down, still buckling his belt or pulling an extra layer of thermal underwear over his head. "Come on," he'd say to Paul, "let's get going," and the two of them would disappear out the door. What Paul gave me, those mornings, was a connection, a warmth I'd rarely felt, and after Jeff went to Montana, it wasn't Jeff I missed, but Paul.

I had a job writing for a magazine, and that meant I had to go out of town every once in a while. Paul loved our dog, Gorm, a brown hound with the face of a golden retriever and the long low body of a basset. He had taken care of her when we'd gone away before, so one day in March I called down there to see if he would take her while I went up north. He sounded pleased and reminded me to bring her dish.

Paul lived in a house that used to be on the main

street, but in 1922, using sleds and four teams of oxen, they moved it to the quiet backstreet neighborhood where it is now. The house was a big rambling Victorian with six gable ends, a slate roof and a wraparound porch with slender, bonelike pillars. The front door was on that porch, but it was never used and the path leading to it was grown over. The paint on the house was once white, I think, but had faded to gray, crinkled like alligator skin. The green shutters were the same. It had a picket fence across the front yard, with a gate that was always open, and in the summer, roses and phlox bloomed in the flower garden that his mother and grandmother used to keep, even though now it was overgrown with years of weeds.

Paul held the house like a secret and I was only invited into it by degrees. When I first knew him, he would greet me on the lawn, and we would stand there and visit. I thought maybe Paul and Arthur lived inside in squalor, but that turned out not to be true. When I was eventually invited in and grew more used to visiting, I always found the kitchen tidy, dishes done, pots in the cupboard and the dining room, which the two of them used as a living room, cluttered only with the newspapers—they read *The Boston Globe* every day as well as the Greenfield paper and sometimes *The Springfield Union* too. For a long time, that was the only part of the house I ever saw, except once Paul took me down cellar to show me where they stored their wood, which they kept in bins like coal; in the fall, they'd slide the chunks through the cellar window from their trucks. And once he took me into the living room to show me a painting his younger sister had done. There was only a couch in there, stacked with folded laundry, and a TV table with cactus-type plants on it. And a rug. I could only assume that his mother had taken most of the furniture out of that room. I knew her piano and organs had been there. They left holes like missing teeth.

On that day, with Gorm on her leash, I went up the steps and knocked. Arthur came to the door. He was a compact man with a pinched, sorrowful face. His eyes were often watery. He almost bowed, opening the door wide. "Come in, come in," he said. And I went into their bare, old-fashioned kitchen. "How about a cup of coffee— it's instant, that's all we have, but how about it?" Without waiting to hear my answer, he pulled a china cup from the cabinet and turned the heat up under the kettle, pushing the jar of coffee crystals toward me. Paul was not around, so when the kettle began to steam I spooned in some granules and poured the hot water into the cup, and Arthur and I settled at chairs on opposite sides of the dining-room table. The big color TV in the corner was on and Willard Scott was smiling and pointing to the map of the United States, though the sound was turned down so his mouth was moving silently.

"The roads are bad now, real bad," Arthur said, referring to the frost heaves that come up that time of year. "You better not go down to the IGA, 'cause if you do you'll never get out. Two cars had to be pulled out of there yesterday. I've been working on the roof over at Blodgett's. Seems good to have the air getting warmer now."

He went on like that, stringing one topic into another, as he's likely to do, until Paul came downstairs. He was rubbing his cheek. "I had to shave," he said, and then knelt and greeted Gorm, who wagged her tail so earnestly that it swung her body side to side. Paul looked up at me. "When will you be back?" he asked.

"I'm not sure," I said. "I'll call you tonight." I got up to leave and Gorm sat still next to Paul.

"Have a safe trip," he said from where he knelt next to Gorm.

I did call him that night, around six, from a Friendly's where I'd stopped to eat. I could hardly hear him. He always spoke so softly on the phone and there was noise in the background from the waitresses and customers. I told him I thought I'd be back around noon the next day and he said, "Gorm and I will be here waiting." When I hung up I had a feeling of warmth inside, just from having made that connection. Even though at that point I'd never been up to his room, I could picture them there. He'd have the radio on and she'd be on the rug, her eyes tight in sleep. This is how he always described it to me.

There was snow that night, so when I got back the next morning I went down to get Gorm and asked Paul if he'd come up and help me shovel the barn roof. He said, "Let's do it right now," and followed me back to the house in his truck. We found a shovel for each of us and angled the ladder onto the roof. Together we climbed up and worked until the shingles were clean of snow. It was Saturday and though it was still midday, I could feel the loneliness of the night coming at me. I asked him if he wanted to go for a walk, and he said sure.

I always felt they were more his woods than mine—

he'd known them since he was a kid. We walked on the crust of the snow into the backwoods—it was a beautiful sunny day and something about being in those woods with him seemed so good and right. Though the winter's snow had begun to let go in the fields, it was still deep where we were walking. Paul pointed to what he said were turkey tracks on the new snow, one splay of feet set right on top of the other, going along in a pretty straight unruffled line. We followed the tracks, ducking under twigs and passing through branches, plunging hip-deep through the crust near the fir trees. "This is what hunting's like," Paul said, smiling back at me as I struggled in his path. "That's why I don't like to hunt."

Pretty soon the tracks became farther apart, as if the bird had been frightened and had picked up the pace. Finally Paul stopped and pointed to some laurels and then looked up into the trees all around us. "He took off," he said, "see that, where he fed on the berries? He's gone. He probably heard us. We shouldn't giggle so much." And he looked at me with all that warmth and I felt connected again and a little afraid. He turned suddenly and said, "It's getting cold. We ought to get back." And we went back over our tracks and came out on the road and walked back down the hill.

We went in for tea and while I put fresh kindling under the lid of the cookstove to urge the kettle to boil and got the mugs out, he said, "Where were you last night, when you called?" He was sitting with his elbow on the table, his chin resting on his palm, his fingertips curled toward his mouth.

"I was at a Friendly's, at a pay phone in the back. Why?"

"I don't know. I could hear all this noise in the background, a lot of people talking. I thought maybe you were at a bar." Then, right away, he started telling me about the steaks he'd bought down at the butcher shop. "I don't know if Arthur's going to Northampton tonight or not." Arthur had been going to visit Paul's mother more and more, a circumstance that was referred to as "going to Northampton." "Maybe when I get home, he'll be gone. Would you . . . do you like steak?"

I hadn't eaten a steak in probably five years, but it sounded good and I said so. He said, "All right, if Arthur's gone when I get home I'll call you up and you can come down and I'll fix steak—I think I've got some string beans, I'm not sure, and fried potatoes." His smile was boyish and excitement built as he mentally planned the menu.

This prospect did sound inviting to me, so oddly comfortable. Just the suggestion and I was already at that table with him, the newspapers pushed off to one side. "If I don't call," he said, "it just means that Arthur didn't go to Northampton."

He didn't call and I spent the evening pacing around, feeling crazy and wondering what kind of weird attraction this was. For one thing, I was married. Even though I knew in my heart that the marriage was over, that made no difference. For another, Paul didn't fit into any category I knew of. Who was he?

·   ·   ·

A few days later Paul called up to ask how my woodpile
was doing. I told him it was getting down there, so he said
he'd be up, probably in the afternoon. When he came, he
got out of his truck and got his saw from the back and went
right to work, cutting up the pile of random-length logs
that were stacked beside the barn. He knew they were too
long for the stove. I put on my jacket and went to help. We
worked together for a while, he doing the cutting and I
doing the splitting, until there was enough to last until
spring, when Jeff would be home.

"I've got a big fire going in my woods," he said, as we
stacked the last of the chunks outside the back door. "I'm
burning up a big pile of tires for my brother. He dumped
them there last summer."

I knew where the pile was, right at the edge of the
woods. "Don't you think you ought to be watching it?" I
asked.

"It can't go anywhere—there's three feet of snow on
the ground!" he said. "But if you want, we can go over."

We went in his truck, straightening the old Indian-
pattern blanket he used to protect the seat before we piled
in, me and Gorm. It was his father's field, where his
brother, Donald, raised hay for his cows. It was only about
a mile down the road from our house.

The tire dump was way at the back of the field, which
is about ten acres, all open and shaped like an *L* but to walk
back to it felt like a mile. The snow still had a good crust, so
we walked along, falling through every once in a while. In
back, near the manure pile from which, for the past several
springs, I had taken manure for my garden, a plume of

thick, yellowish smoke was rising up through the trees. Donald had dumped tires, about fifty of them, in a gorge at the edge of the field. Part of the pile was out in the open, but there were small trees growing out of the pit and lots of overhanging branches near the wet, smoldering pile.

"See," he said, "it isn't much of a fire. I had trouble getting it started, what with the snow and all." He'd nabbed a bag full of papers off my porch and he threw it into the center, where a tiny flame flickered beneath all the smoke. In order to see the fire, I had to go to the edge of the bank—the icy crust sloped down in a soft, steep curve—and peer in. I felt as if I might just slide into the flame on the soles of my rubber boots, so I stood back, but Paul went right to the edge and squatted down, watching the smoke pump up from the crevice.

I heard the paper bag go up with a *pooooff*, then an angry crackling, followed by a *ping*, like an inner tube popping inside a tire. The flames got thicker and the smoke turned richly black and came up out of the gorge as if it were being cranked from a huge machine. It wrapped itself around the branches overhead and the wind picked up and first pushed it away from us and then pulled it back, so we had to dodge. The smoke and the cold sent tears running from the corners of my eyes.

Paul and I stood motionless a long time, watching the flames move and grow under the snow.

Several branches overhead were waving as if from gusts of wind, but it was from the heat; a felled log beside the gorge had begun to smolder. Can there be fires when there is snow on the ground? I didn't have any idea, but I could easily imagine the treetops igniting from the intensity of this fire. We didn't even have a shovel. I tried to imagine how the fire trucks would ever get in to the spot, where the trees linked directly to several houses that were couched in the woods. The snow was so deep under the crust only snowmobiles could make it.

"Is this okay?" I ventured.

Paul disregarded my shyly expressed concern. "It's not going anywhere," was all he said. I was freezing from standing so long, my feet nearly numb in spite of my insulated boots and heavy socks. Snow flurries were starting, thin against the white sky and the white-white field. I bobbed a little, hopping up and down on my toes, to make the feeling come back.

"I'll take you home," he said and we both whistled for Gorm, who'd wandered off into the woods, and finally she came along and we walked back across the long field, so bright it blinded me, made my eyes dance. "Won't be long," he said, "till we're out here riding up and down on the tractor, raking hay."

Back at the house, I pushed the coals together in the stove and put some of the chunks we'd split on top and settled into the rocker to thaw. I started reading from the stack of newspapers that had piled up over the week, but the memory of the fire, the way the flames had begun to reach up from under the snow, kept coming back at me.

I got up and put on my hat and two more pairs of clean socks and an extra sweater. I got a shovel and a dry pair of work gloves from the barn. Gorm hopped into the car with me and I drove back to the field.

By then the snow was coming in a hard, straight line and I couldn't see to the end of the field, where I'd half expected to see flames across the sky, spreading into the pines so close to the tire dump. As I got closer, using the shovel to steady me on the crust slippery with new snow, I looked for Paul. I couldn't see him—had he slipped down into the fire?—but I finally spotted his red plaid hat. He was squatting at the edge of the ravine, his hands jammed into his jacket pockets, staring down into the fire. Bright orange flames raced up out of the tires. I called out and he seemed startled, turning to face me, as if waking out of a dream.

He broke into a grin when he saw me, armed with my shovel. "Looks like those flaming hoops that the lions jump through at the circus, doesn't it?" he said, pointing into the gorge.

"Paul," I said, "don't you think you ought to trim it back a little?"

He laughed. "Oh, Edie, Edie, Edie," he said, as if to a child, "look at this." He took the shovel and dug into the snow, chipping beneath the crust to open it up, like a hole in the ice. He threw heaping shovelsful onto a piece of tire that had fallen farther down into the gorge, very near the smoldering tree. The flames hissed and then burst back, hissed and steamed and flew open again until he hit the tire dead center with a hunk of snow. The flames died. "See," he said, handing the shovel back to me, "it can't go anywhere."

I fell into Paul's trance, feeling fear mixed with excitement as each new tire burst into flames from under the snow, a magician's trick that made the snow vanish.

I stuck the shovel into the snow and went over to the edge and squatted next to him. It was warm there and he had his jacket unzipped. I watched the brilliant flames rip out of the gorge, being drawn further and further into the brightness. The sticks and twigs that jutted up out of the snow were burning. The branches overhead were soot-black and steaming.

"I think I've got a couple of other tires back in the shed," he said, after some time had passed. "Let's go get them." The snow was coming down fast enough to pile up on our hats and shoulders. Our footprints were gone by the time we walked back to the shed, on the other side of the field. He crawled in over the hay rake and manure spreader and picked his way to the back.

"Aha!" his voice came out from inside. "I've got more than just a couple—look at this one!" It was a tractor tire, tall as my shoulders and he rolled it out, wobbling, over the snow at me, following it with two more bald truck tires. We rolled them back and threw them into the fire— the big one we heaved in together, *one, two, threee!*—and they bounced down into the center of the fire. They took almost at once and turned into flaming O's, just like he'd said, like a lion's challenge at the circus.

The fire was burning in the shape of a *V,* with most of the flames on the right, but thick yellow smoke was beginning to boil out of the opening in the snow, and pretty soon the spot where he'd dug was steaming like a kettle. My guard went back up. "God, Paul, this is all burning up under the snow, the fire is under us!" I moved off to a distance, imagining the snow would suddenly open beneath us like a trapdoor and drop us into the fire. I took the shovel and began to throw snow down into the pit, where the flames seemed mysteriously bottomless.

"Hey!" Paul called. I looked over at him and our eyes met. "It's my fire," he said, very quietly.

He was right. I didn't know why I'd come back there. I heard sirens in the distance. The firemen must be coming to search for the source of this thick black smoke coming up out of the woods. I felt my cheeks burning against the cold. I felt embarrassed. "I'm heading back," I said, trying to sound nonchalant. "My feet are getting cold again." When I left, there were still dozens of tires inside the *V* that had not caught yet.

It was almost dark by then, anyway. When I got to my car, parked up against the snowbank at the edge of the field, I listened again for the sirens but didn't hear any. The snow had stopped and the full moon had come out and made the new snow sparkle.

When I went to bed that night, tacking towels up over the windows to keep the moonlight out, I wondered if Paul was still there, squatting next to the fire that came up out of the bright new snow. I wondered if the fire trucks had come. When I closed my eyes, hot orange O's flared up on the backs of my eyelids. I dreamt that I went back to find Paul, and the woods were blazing, that same petroleum-bright orange, moving fast against the still, white snow, but I couldn't find Paul. I went down to his house, I went to the neighbor's barn, I went to the shed at the other side of the field. Everywhere I went, heavy black smoke pumped angrily out of the doors and windows, but I couldn't find Paul anywhere.

A couple of days later, he came up.

"The fire's still burning. I've just been out there," he said. "But almost all the tires are gone now."

It seemed impossible, since both days had been gray and drizzly.

"Did the fire trucks ever come?" I asked.

He gave me one of those looks, a little amused. "Nope."

That day spent watching the fire came back to me, over and over. What fascinated me then was the smoldering fire under that cold winter landscape and how Paul fed it with such confidence and certainty.

I went away again in the spring, up to the Connecticut lakes for a story I was writing about the river. Jeff was still not back. Gorm stayed with Paul and when I got home I went down to pick her up. It was Sunday night, late, around nine, which was usually about Paul's and his father's bedtime but they had just come back from his brother Donald's farm, where they both spent a lot of time, helping with chores. Paul was making bacon sandwiches because they'd missed dinner while they did the milking. I stood in the small kitchen and chatted with him as he poked the strips of meat around in the black skillet with a three-pronged fork. Arthur moved around us. I told Paul about the moose I'd seen along the roadsides up there.

"I've never seen a moose," Paul said. "I'd like to some-day."

He put the fork on the counter and stooped down, taking Gorm's head in his hands. "Gorm was good," he said, rubbing her forehead with his thumb. Her eyes half closed in pleasure. "I'll miss her."

I usually baked something for him, something sweet to return his favor, so I asked what he'd like this time.

"Say," Arthur butted in, "do you know how to make a rhubarb pie?"

"Sure."

"We've got the rhubarb," said Arthur. "You just make the pie."

When I went to get the rhubarb the next day, Paul was already outside on the front lawn, kneeling next to the huge clump of rhubarb, cutting the long stalks with a kitchen knife and putting them in a brown-paper bag. I'd brought a basket and I joined him. The rhubarb was huge, the leaves the size of dinner plates, the stalks nearly a yard long. "This is just the small patch," he said, cutting a final stalk and putting it in the bag. "The good ones are down by the chicken house."

It wasn't just the house that I loved, but the grounds around it. It was a small plot, probably not more than an acre. There was the chicken house, where they had twenty or thirty chickens when Paul was growing up, and the shed, where Donald kept his cow, and the gardens, and every imaginable fruit and vegetable—blackberries, butter-nuts, apples, pears, lilacs, rhododendrons, and in front of the chicken house some of the biggest, brightest holly-hocks I'd ever seen. We went down to the chicken house and sure enough, all along the back edge was rhubarb, stretching out its green leaves like open palms. We cut and cut until the brown bag was full and the basket, which was big enough to carry an infant in, was piled to the handle and hard to carry. He said we could cut all I could use, that they wouldn't use it. "She used to come and cut it, make a pie for us from some of what she cut," he said, meaning his mother, "but she hasn't done that, the past couple of years."

I like to cut up rhubarb and freeze it raw, make pies when the snow is high outside. I told him that I'd make him another pie, in return for this harvest, maybe in the wintertime. "Yes," he said, "make it when it's twenty below."

Paul took the basket and carried it with two hands and I took the bag, which burst with the green and pink stalks, and we walked back up the hill to my car. Next to the house he put the basket down and said, "Come here, I want to show you something." I followed him around to the front porch. He pointed up to the little piece of ornate gingerbread that braced one of the pillars. "A robin," he said and there was a nest in the crotch, and when we came near, the mother flew away and I said, "Let's go get a step-ladder and look at the eggs," but he said no, we better leave it alone until they hatch. We watched it for a moment. The robin didn't come back.

The porch, though it was narrow and had no screens,

looked out across tall trees and onto hills that were greeny blue in the distance. It was bare, just a painted floor.

I said, "Oh, Paul, you should have a chair out here. Wouldn't it be nice to sit here and watch the sky go black?"

He leaned against the narrow pillar, looking out to the hills.

"Mmmm."

Next to the porch were more flowers. The old gardens, overgrown with weeds, still held iris, ready to bloom, and peonies that seemed lush even in the witchgrass. There were beautiful tiny blue flowers, a little like violets, scattered outside the overgrown borders and I leaned close and looked through the higher growth to find evidence of other possibilities—daffodils and lilies and poppies and ajuga. I pointed out each one, amazed. "There is so much hidden here," I said.

"Yes," he said, "she used to keep it weeded and there was something of everything." He went over to the huge, billowing rhododendron that grew next to the porch and picked one of the blooms that had just begun to open. "She started this from a cutting she took from a bush on Pine Street." He stretched out his hand, offering me the deep violet flower. "Put this in your hair," he said.

Jeff was coming home in three days. I had an assignment to do in New York before he came back. I was looking forward to it. Spring in New York is pretty nice. I called Paul to see if he would look after Gorm while I was gone.

He answered on the fifth ring. "Hello," he said.

"Hi," I said, "it's me. Could you take care of Gorm for a couple of days? I have to go to New York."

"New York City?" he asked.

"Have you ever been to New York City?" I asked. There was a silence.

"No."

"Want to come?" I said it almost without thinking.

Another silence. I filled it with the information he probably wanted. "It's not really overnight. I take the train down. It leaves Brattleboro at one o'clock in the morning and gets into New York at seven A.M. I do what I need to do and then I catch the nine o'clock evening train back home. It gets into Brattleboro at three in the morning. I like it because I don't have to get a room that way—that's so expensive—but I get a full day in the city anyhow." I felt as if I was trying to sell him on it. I really wasn't, but I thought it would be fun, taking Paul to a place so unlike anything he'd ever seen. "I usually get a little sleep on the train," I went on.

He still didn't say anything. "A ticket costs forty dollars. That's for both ways," I said.

Finally he said, "Maybe Arthur could take care of Gorm."

That sounded a little complicated.

"Maybe we could leave her with some extra food, tied to her house. It's warm enough outside now."

"Yes," he said. "Let's do that."

"Can you come up here, around midnight?" I asked.

"Sure," he said. This time his voice was strong.

• • •

After supper I got dressed and ready to go and then lay on the couch. I wanted to sleep a little, but my mind wouldn't shut down. If I looked at it one way, this was a crazy thing to do. But New York was so much a part of me. Though I'd chosen to live far from that city, all my grandparents were born there and my grandfather ran a business just around the corner from Wall Street. Every Saturday, when I was growing up, he took me with him into the city on the train. As teenagers, my friends and I would feel grown-up, riding the train into Penn Station and taking the bus down Fifth Avenue to the Village. We'd sit in the dark coffeehouses, drink bitter drinks, and listen to young long-haired musicians sing brave songs about love and about freedom.

It was almost as if I were taking Paul home, to see my turf. I knew he'd never seen anything like it. And he had a way of mirroring his feelings in his face, without using words. I drifted into sleep, imagining the look on his face when we got off the train. I had set the alarm for 12:00 but I woke up not to the alarm but to a tapping on the back door.

"You're early," I said, turning on the lights and letting him in. Under his red-and-black-checked lumber jacket, he had on a white shirt and dark pants. His hair was combed, with water or oil, I couldn't tell which, like a choirboy's.

The streets were empty in Brattleboro and I parked up the hill from the station. We walked down through the cool night to the station house, which is huge, a stone building with lots of levels for loading and unloading freight. The Amtrak was the only train that stopped there anymore. Down around back is a little beat-up door with a light over the top, the only part of the station left that has anything to do with trains. At the door was a rotund man wearing a square-topped railroad cap and a mussed-up Amtrak jacket. He was leaning up against the stone façade, smoking a pipe in a deliberate sort of way, watching us out of the corner of his eye. There were no other passengers waiting. That was not unusual. "Guess it's just us," I said to Paul and he looked at me hard and said, "Good."

The station man kept smoking and didn't look at us.

"Is the train going to be on time?" I asked. I had taken it often enough to know it would be unusual if it were.

"Couldn't tell you," he said, without looking at me.

The moon was just past full, still bright enough to seem like a streetlight against the dark sky.

It was getting chilly, so the man unlocked the door and let us inside to the waiting room, where the straight-back chairs were stacked on top of one another like a closed lunchroom. I took a chair from the pile, picked up an old *People* magazine and leafed through it. Paul took a chair too, and sat down.

"Cold," I said and pulled my jacket tight around me.

Paul pulled his chair close to mine. "Lean in," he said and I did, feeling his warmth.

"I think we've got it," the station man called to us and we jumped up and went outside to the platform. We could hear the distant whistle, a cry that came closer as the big shiny aluminum engine bore down on us, the tracks tapping underneath. There were a dozen or more cars and Paul went up close to the tracks. He looked intently up into the sleeping cars that loped past us. The cars were softly lit inside and we could see, in nightlight twilight, the restless sleep of its passengers. The sleepers passed and then the lounge cars ambled past, the insomniacs and the drinkers gazing blankly out into the blackness that was us. Then the dining car, the tables set with the prim white cloths and single bud vases, ready for the breakfast crowd. The train stopped so that the last two cars were even with the platform and our station man, whose straight, greasy hair straggled out from under his cap like spikes in the light of the train, didn't offer his assistance as we boarded, but after we were up there said, "Have a good time, now." And he waved the train free of the station with his hand lantern, a beam no brighter than a flashlight.

We settled into a couple of seats. Paul was looking around him, a little lost.

"Haven't you been on a train before?"

"No, never," he said.

"Sit by the window." He scooted past me and sank into the oversized seat, turning to face the night.

I couldn't imagine it. When I was growing up in New Jersey, trains linked the towns and I often took the train, even when I was very little, to visit my grandparents, three towns away. My mom would put me on and tell me to count three stations and my grandmother would be waiting on the cement platform of the Summit station, some forty-five minutes later. I told this to Paul.

"In high school, I used to go into New York with friends, to Greenwich Village. . . ."

"Look," he said, pointing out the dark window. It was the Vernon nuclear power plant, lit up like a small city, the eerie orange lights reflected in the river. Then Puffer's truck depot, lit only with a street light.

The door at the end of the car *whooshed* open and a conductor steadied himself on it, letting in the sounds of our speed clattering along the tracks. Cold night air pushed in with him. He wobbled down the darkened aisle toward us and asked us where we were going. "Penn Station," I said and Paul flashed me a grin of anticipation. The train-man punched our tickets and stuck them on the seat ahead of us as we fished in our wallets for the cash. I asked him why the train was so late, and he said that, since the floods, the tracks had been undercut with water so they had to go half speed. I could feel it as he said it, the train rocking back and forth like a boat in swells.

"We've been running about an hour late for a couple of weeks now," he said, "but we try to make it up once we get past New Haven."

He moved on toward the next car, using the seat backs for handholds as he went. When he left, Paul pulled the torn canvas shade down to block out the pulse of street-lights that flashed on and off as we moved. The car was almost completely dark.

"Are you cold?" he asked.

"Yes," I said, "freezing."

He stood up and took off his jacket and sat back down, close in. He laid the jacket across both of us like a blanket. We cranked the seats back and our shoulders touched. Under the jacket he found my hand and captured it. I set my head on his shoulder, and in the creeping, wallowing motion dropped off to sleep.

I slept only about an hour. I looked up and Paul's eyes were open, looking at me. I smiled. "Go to sleep," I said.

He smiled back and said, "I have been."

I drifted off again, soothed by the motion and by his warmth. It was a short night, only another hour before the sun came in from under the shade. I reached past Paul and pinched the catch and pushed it up. We were probably somewhere in Connecticut. The landscape of junkyards and carpet outlets and the backs of triple-deckers looked somehow magical in the new orange light.

Paul was wide awake, sitting up, watching out the window as the scenery whizzed past. He was eating from the package of licorice he'd stashed in his pocket before we left. The train was still empty, which seemed to me to be very rare, so we talked without restraint, pointing out parts of the painting that passed before us. The cement-block walls of factories were cluttered with spray-painted messages that were hard to read and even the words we could make out, we couldn't understand. Wild roses grew up from the track bed, rising like an apology against the chain-link fences that wrapped around junkyards.

"Look." Paul sat up and pointed to a car hulk, trunk and hood yawning, tires gone, doors gone, slumped next to the tracks with the roses, sweet pink blooms, twined up around its paint-flecked skin.

We settled back again as the new sun angled in. By

now the train was racing, the tracks under us making staccato the old rhyme, *fiddle-dee-dee, fiddle-dee-dee, fiddle-dee-dah, fiddle-dee-dah, fiddle-dee-dee, fiddle-dee-dee,* like a record on the wrong speed.

"We'll probably be there in an hour or so," I said. He gave my hand a little squeeze. He hadn't let go all night.

"Can't wait," he said.

2

What I learned from taking Paul to New York was perhaps more about myself than about him. He enjoyed the trip. Since the train gets in so early in the morning and doesn't leave again until nine at night, it makes for a long day. We went to the auction I had to write about. It was at Christie's, where the auction itself is more like a social event, almost as different as you could get from the cattle auctions and Monday-night auctions Paul liked to drop in on at home. We ate hot pastrami sandwiches (he had never heard of pastrami) at a noisy deli and we entered into the hushed calm of Saint Patrick's Cathedral, whose ceilings were higher than any he had ever seen, maybe even imagined, and on our way back to the station we walked down Park

Avenue and ducked into the lobby of the Waldorf-Astoria, where we sat on the blue velvet cushions near the center fountain. The place sparkled around us like some sort of fairyland.

"My great-grandfather and -grandmother lived here," I told him, hope dimming that I could impress him.

"Hmmm," he said, his eyes following the dressed-up couples who paraded past us, on their way to night entertainment.

"In fact, my great-grandfather died here," I went on, my thoughts opening up to a story my aunt had once told me. "He had a mistress named Mabel. She knew he was dying and she sat down here in the lobby, crying." Paul turned to me fully now. "Supposedly my great-grandfather was saying her name, calling for her as he died. My great-grandmother knew she was down here but she wouldn't let her come up to the room and he died without seeing her."

Paul's eyes turned soft, full of the feeling I was beginning to know he was capable of. "That's really sad," he said.

We left the Waldorf and walked toward the station, holding hands like two children along the wide, grand sidewalk. At that time of night, the sidewalks are mostly empty except for an occasional couple, glitzed up and ready for the show. We walked down, Grand Central Station getting bigger and bigger, cabs whizzing past us at great speed, their tires crashing into the holes in the crumbling pavement. Every taxi that passed us was filled with theatergoers or couples on their way somewhere on that dreamy Saturday night. I spotted one arrowing toward us, empty, and stuck my hand up. The driver was Chinese and we huddled in the back while the cab hurtled down Park and through the tunnel under Grand Central and on down to Penn Station, where the streets were clogged with people, people everywhere, a striking contrast to the near-solitude of Park Avenue. "Where did everyone come from?" Paul asked, looking around at the sea of faces.

The train was an hour late getting in, and when it finally did there was a huge crowd clumped along the platform, waiting to get on. It seemed as if every seat was taken by the time we boarded. We walked back and back until we found a car where there were two seats together and settled into them, snugging together against the coolness of the evening. Paul fished in his pocket and brought out the half-eaten package of licorice he'd been working on that morning. He gave me half, and we ate as we watched the train fill up even more. A black man, broad and tall, strode down the aisle to the only other empty seat, which was across from us. He had on silky red jogging shorts with a leather belt that slung loose down to his groin. The belt buckle spelled HARD in brass letters. He wore leather gloves that left his fingers free, like golf or biking gloves, but at each knuckle there was a steel spike. To match, it seemed, he had a leather bracelet, which fit tight to his wrist, studded with steel bolts. He carried an oversized duffel and when he got his long legs settled in the double seat, he drew a tall can of Old Milwaukee out of the duffel, popped the top and drank it down in one long gulp.

Paul and I watched this together, as if we were watching a movie, and when the man crushed the empty can beneath his booted foot, Paul turned to me with a look that mixed astonishment with amusement. He reached his arm around me and took my shoulder and pulled me close. His chest felt solid and strong, and I let my head go down against it. The train gave a sigh and began to move, a soft, floating feeling as if we were being set adrift. The windows were black and the lights were turned low. We tipped our heads against each other and, in the rhythm of the train, we slept.

If I had not been married to Jeff and if Paul had not been working with him, I suppose this would have been the beginning of a courtship, albeit an odd one. But my life was still so tangled with Jeff and all that we had built into our lives. Paul continued to work with Jeff and what bound the triangle was loyalty, Paul's loyalty to Jeff, so like that to his father, and my own loyalty to Jeff, which makes little sense to me now except that I believed then that a marriage was forever and that you did what you could to make it work.

Soon after this Jeff came home, and he and Paul fell back into working together. A wall of tension grew up between me and Paul—we didn't know what to say to each other, how to leap the chasm we'd opened in the time we'd spent together while Jeff was away.

For me and Jeff, the hope of repairing our marriage seemed very dim. There was no love. We accepted that. Yet the structure of our lives, so invested in our house and all the work that it had meant for us, made separation so hard. We had removed ourselves from the mainstream to such a degree that separation from each other would mean removing ourselves from the subculture we'd settled into so thoroughly. Confusion was part of my life, a steady background noise, but in spite of it the underlying and increasingly persistent passion for Paul overwhelmed everything else. Yet his oddness, the disparity of our lives and in our selves, deterred me. How could I be in love with a man like that? It didn't fit any mold I could think of. I confided in a friend who lived far away, told her of this fascination, and she listened sympathetically yet finally she concluded, "Well, these things never work out, you know."

So Jeff and I continued in our patterns. In the early part of the summer, we bought a tiny Cape, a very old cottage in the woods out in a village called Chesham, quite a distance north of us. This house was to become my refuge from Jeff, but when we bought it, it was purely a profit-making venture. The roof on it swayed till I wondered why it didn't snap and the sills were so rotted they came out in our hands like peat moss. But it was sweet, small and simple, shaped like one of the little wooden houses on the Monopoly board, the chimney in the center, two big windows on either side of the front door, which was red. I could easily see it fixed up, gardens planted where now there were rusted car parts and ancient electric stoves rooted in the soft black earth. We bought it for the price of the land and planned to fix it up, on spec. We planned to do most of the labor ourselves, which was how we had worked so often in the past, and to hire Paul for some of the detail. We started that summer, tearing down the walls, peeling the shingles off the crumbling roof. I took vacation time for this, and worked over in Chesham every day.

It is a dirty job, pulling down an old house. I bought a blue work suit, like garage mechanics wear. On our first day in Chesham, Jeff showed me how to get started. I got into my suit, which was big enough to fit over my clothes, wrapped my hair in a red bandanna, pulled on work gloves, and the dust mask. Jeff was dressed almost identically. We were standing in what would be the living room. The big windows with their small panes of wavy glass looked out on the trees that grew in close, close enough so their leaves touched the glass.

"Use the shovel like this." Jeff reared back, swinging the shovel like a baseball bat; he smashed the wall and smashed the wall, leaving only dents and veins in the tough plaster. I stepped back to avoid the cloud of dust. He leaned the shovel against the wall and picked the long crowbar out of his toolbox. "Once you've got it started," he said, his voice distorted from behind the mask, "take the bar and start to pull the plaster off the lath, smash it and pull it off until it's just the lath." The clouds of dust were so thick I could hardly see him, but when the air cleared he handed me the shovel and the bar and went in to do the kitchen, calling, "Start with the ceiling."

It had probably been thirty years since anyone had painted the walls. The odd pastel colors, light blue and green, were faded and striped darkly with soot at each section of lath. The plaster was a thin skin, mixed with horsehair to make it stronger. Standing on one of the two chairs left in the house, I took the shovel and bashed at the ceiling. The shovel bounced back at me. Hardly a nick. I tried again, harder, and plaster rained and dust filled the

room. I smashed at it some more and with the plaster
spilled down tiny toys, tin cars no bigger than house keys,
marbles, Golden Books soggy with time, a Halloween
mask, corncobs, acorn shells, a cotton bra with white metal
hooks for fasteners, a baby's slipper. With each swipe, I
brought down a fresh windfall, and when the dust cleared,
I stooped to inspect, sifting through the rocks of plaster,
and I squirreled away the few treasures in a paper cup: a
green plastic soldier, his rifle aimed; a red metal taxicab
with the driver painted on the side; a cat's-eye marble. Paul
told me later that mice or rats, maybe squirrels, must have
taken them up there. They seemed to have a vintage, as if
everything had been stashed away sometime in the fifties.
They were toys such as I had when I was growing up.

Every once in a while I stopped and watched Jeff in
the next room, leaping at the ceiling with his bar and then
standing back as the ceiling crashed all around him. We had
worked on so many jobs together with a single purpose.
The purpose now seemed obscure. The suit, the odd mask
Jeff wore and the bar he wielded made him look like a
terrorist, a madman in the gray-brown dust made rich by
the sunlight that came through the window.

We worked for a couple of days, shoveling the lath
and plaster down a chute outside the windows. When we'd
finished, I swept the corners, and the crooked, ancient pine
floors, dusted off the cookstove and brushed the last traces
of nutshells and sawdust off the cross braces. I stood back
and admired the bare bones of the old house, the color of
the beams much like new wood. I thought of Paul. I
thought of him constantly, but didn't know how to get to

him. I had seen him only once since the spring. I asked him to come out and see this house, before we bought it. I wanted his opinion. We'd driven over in his truck, Gorm on the seat between us.

"I really like this," he'd said, when we got there. He put about as much expression as you can get into those little words. He hopped out of his truck and began to poke around.

"It's got a lot of possibilities, don't you think?" I asked him, searching.

"Yup," he said and went about the business of crawling under the joists and up into the knee walls, checking the timbers, smelling the air for trouble.

We weren't out there for very long, just long enough for him to go through the house. "It's so small," he said as we drove home, "but it would make a good home for two people who love each other."

I had forgotten the pleasure of riding with him. He drove the truck along at a leisurely pace, pointing out things on the roadside, a barn that had fallen in, a flock of black hens scratching in a mean-looking dooryard, an old man smoking a big cigar, things I would have passed by without seeing. When we got home Jeff was not there, so Paul came in and we read the paper together at the kitchen table. When the sun grew strong on the porch we went out and circled the garden, checking the rhubarb for a second picking, counting out the iris against the stone wall. "A good time for a nap," he said, lying down on the grass bank that sloped away from the garden. I stretched out next to him. He put his hat, stained with bug dope, over his face and folded his arms across his stomach. I turned to look at him. He looked back for a long minute and then, before I could say anything, he was on his feet, walking up to his truck. As he drove down the road he tooted a little song on his horn, and Gorm ran after him, all the way to the tree line.

Jeff and Paul continued to work at the little Chesham house. I sometimes drove over and ate lunch with them, sat on a sawhorse and watched them. The poetry of Paul's work continued to fascinate me. I was almost mesmerized by it. One day I found Jeff in a curt humor, not even looking up when I came in, pushing past me saying he was pressed for time when I tried to make conversation. So I sat with Paul and watched him frame a door and when Jeff half-jokingly told me to "stop bothering the help" and go back to work, Paul raised his voice uncharacteristically and pointed at me, saying, "You stay right there!"

Even so, I left. When he came home that night, Jeff said, strongly, "Please don't come around anymore. After you left, Paul went into a trance and he was just about worthless." The next day he came home even more upset. "Christ," he said, rummaging in the drawer for some rolling papers, "the guy's *gone*. He was putting up the clapboards *backward*. He must be trying to sabotage the job or something."

Paul was the one who taught Jeff how to clapboard. Paul in fact taught Jeff much of what he knew. Comments from Jeff about Paul's strangeness were common enough for me not to listen to them all that much.

The next day I was supposed to go to Maine, but plans shifted, so at lunch I went over to tell Jeff I'd be home for supper after all. I'd intended to just deliver my message and then leave, but Paul came into the room like a ghost, hovering at the door, his face white as chalk, his eyes red and shrouded.

"Paul," I said, trying not to reflect alarm, "are you sick?"

"I'm okay," he said. His voice was hoarse and barely audible.

I went in and told Jeff I would be home that night and then left through the hallway, where I stopped and took Paul's arm and said, "Take care of yourself." He pulled his mouth into a flat line, meant to be a smile, and I guess he meant to say *uh-huh* but it came out more like a moan. His eyes were full of pain.

I went back to work and fell into a trance of my own. While Jeff might think Paul was goofing-off or daydreaming or even sabotaging, I knew there was more than that going on.

I went to sleep trying to erase that look I'd seen in Paul's eyes. I felt frightened for him. In the morning, Jeff said, "If the fucking guy is ten minutes late, I'm going without him." Paul had been coming ten, fifteen, twenty minutes late—Paul who always came fifteen minutes early, full of cheer. The time came and passed. Jeff waited out by his truck. After half an hour, Paul drove slowly up the road, very slowly. From the kitchen window I saw him get out and go over to Jeff's truck, his steps slow and careful. I heard Jeff say, "We're going to be on a roof today and you know you can't go up there feeling the way you do."

A few minutes later, Jeff came inside. "Paul's going to stay here. He doesn't want to go home. He's just going to putter around in the shop. Just leave him alone," he said, giving me a kiss on the neck and rushing out the door.

I had an office over Jeff's shop in the barn. I did most of my writing there. After I got the kitchen cleaned up I went over and started at my typewriter. I could hear Paul below me, pacing, so I went down. He was standing behind the table saw as if it were a fort. The light was dim, but I was sure he was trembling; in any case, his eyes were deep red. I tried to go near him but he backed away like a frightened animal.

"What's wrong?" I asked, as softly as I could.

He shrugged and turned sideways and then said, each word an eternity, "I'm scared about my life."

I tried again to go over to him, but I could see him stiffen, so I just said, "Come on up to my office and we can talk."

He walked around the saw and up the stairs as if he were being led on a string. I pulled the wicker chair around to face the couch and offered him tea—peppermint, which he liked.

"What is it that's scaring you, Paul?"

He sat still as a stone, staring straight ahead. After a while, I asked him again, and he finally pushed his hands out in front of him and said, his face distorted with an unmistakable pain, "I feel like I'm in a big bowl of trouble," each word coming out separately and very slowly.

I asked him if anything had happened, and he said no. He stared when I asked him if he was having trouble sleeping.

Finally I said, "Paul, do you know how much I care about you?"

And he said, very quickly, "Yes, I know."

"Is that what's wrong?"

"I don't know," he said, very softly.

And I said, "I want to help. What can I do to help?" But he didn't answer, he just stared. I kept thinking that he was mulling over in his mind just how he was going to answer, but time passed and he said nothing, his eyes brimming with tears that never fell, tears that sat in a pool on the brink of his lower lids.

He drank his tea and we sat and I looked at him, and every once in a while he turned his wretched eyes on me and I'd think he was going to say something but he'd finally just turn them away, back to the floor or to his palms, resting in his lap.

"I feel like nothing could be worse," he said at last.

"What?" I asked.

Minutes passed. "Like what could be worse?" I asked again.

There was no response. I had heard from various people that Paul had spent a month in a psychiatric ward when he was in high school. I didn't know the reasons, but I knew that for Paul this was a source of shame. I don't think he knew that I knew. It struck a chord with me. I too had been a "difficult" child in school. I was filled with anger and had been sent to psychiatrists at various times because of my aggressive behavior. I had a breakdown on my twentieth birthday, and ended up in a psychiatric ward for a couple of weeks. Though I know it isn't the answer to all troubles, I felt that there were two things that helped me get beyond that warp. One was to take responsibility for my life, which I did, after a lot of hard lessons. The other was to love and to be loved. For that, I still searched. I had played by the rules much more adeptly than Paul, that is to say, to the casual observer I seemed much more normal, but inside I identified deeply with him, with his attempt to keep his balance within a world he didn't fully connect with. It was much easier for me to guess all this about him than it was for him to see it in me. I wanted to find a way to tell him.

"Paul, what about talking with someone, a psychiatrist, maybe. Would you talk to one—I could arrange it for you."

"Yes," he said at last.

So I got out the phone book to try to think of who, and then called Max, a man I had first seen as a counselor and to whom Jeff and I had gone together for marriage counseling. I still saw him, off and on. He was OK for the kinds of things Jeff and I were bringing to him, but I didn't think he was quite up to what Paul needed. I thought he might be able to recommend someone, but when I explained the situation and asked whom he might suggest, he let out, "What about me?" in a rather offended tone so I covered the receiver and asked Paul if he'd like to talk to Max and he said OK. Max scheduled Paul for his first available appointment.

It was still early. I had work to do, but I felt I needed to stay with Paul. I wanted to plant onions in the garden, so I invited him to come with me to Agway to buy the sets. It sounded OK to him, I guess, since, though he didn't answer, he drifted up toward my car and got in on the passenger side. We drove to Brattleboro. He sat like a statue, his eyes glazed, set straight ahead. In the car his smell was stronger, waves of humid heat coming off him, not offensive, just strong, a mix of damp cotton, some kind of sweet-smelling deodorant and the heat and tension of his body.

When I got out to go inside, he got out along with me. He stayed next to me, just as close as he could get without touching. I wanted to put my arms around him and hold on to him, keep him from falling, but I was afraid of upsetting the balance. When he stood beside the counter I held on to his shoulders from behind and rested my hand on his back as we walked, not knowing if this was an invasion but needing somehow to support him, however slightly.

He stayed still like that and stared, saying nothing, all the way home. When we reached home and got out of the car, I felt the frustration of it all, all this time, the great chasm that had opened between us since Jeff had come home, of things unsaid, feelings unspoken. As we walked toward the garden, I stopped next to the new row of beans and said, "Paul! I'm not helping you! What is it? Talk to me. Tell me what is wrong!" I grabbed his arm and held on to it, afraid he would pull back, but he stayed there, his eyes coming to rest on mine. In my mind, as all this unfolded, I kept thinking that somehow I was at fault. I wondered if all this hadn't been a big tease for him. I couldn't bear to look at him like that—his hair was matted with sweat, he was white as a sheet and his eyes had been tearing all day, leaving a thick crust of "sleep" along the edge of his lower lids. When I got close to him I could see that he had tried to shave that morning but had missed more than half his beard, which seemed to twirl in every direction. I knew that at times he was all I thought about: was I messing up his life this badly? I kept a tight hold and said, "Paul, how do you feel about me?"

While Jeff had been away in Montana, Paul and I could talk about almost anything. Since he'd returned, we'd sunk back into silence; we could only talk about simple things. It was something that we had lost and I knew we both felt this. It hung heavy all around us.

He turned his eyes away from mine and looked down at the little bean plants that had just emerged the day before. Finally he said, his voice hoarse and ragged and tiny, "I like you."

"Paul, do I have anything to do with this?"

He stood still and stared back. He said nothing.

I plunged on, anxious to let him know how I felt, to come clean with all this.

"Paul!" I'd started to cry. "I have feelings for you that I probably shouldn't have. But they're not wrong, Paul, believe me, they're not wrong." I put my arm around his neck to give him a hug and he put his arm around my waist, drawing me to him, holding on to my shoulder with his other hand, not pushing me away but holding me there, so that we ended up in an embrace that was more like a dance, our eyes locked.

Finally I let go, saying, "Let's plant the onions."

We did, and for every ten bulbs I put in, Paul put in one, moving in excruciatingly slow motion. When we'd put in five rows, I said, "How about some lunch?" And he moved wordlessly up onto the porch and into the kitchen.

I was certain that his life was at stake. Everyone needs a reason to live. My reasoning was in a sense saying that love was going to make him weak, not strong, when all the religions of the world, all the wisdom since time began, say the opposite. Which led me down the path of: is this the wrong kind of love? I didn't know what kind it was—just trying to define it got sticky and damp and not something I wanted to follow through. I have known people who use mental illness as a way to get love, but Paul's dark moods were always something I thought he tried to hide. I'd often sensed them, but his efforts to conceal them were so convincing that I was sure that they were very dark and not something he could summon when he was feeling hungry for love. Anyway, I was in it too deep to turn back. Long ago I'd held out my hand to him for a friendship I wanted and at times encouraged beyond what I thought he was willing to give. I wanted to make him come alive! What was sitting in front of me was the complete opposite. I was desperate, devastated, certain that if I didn't do the exact right thing I would lose him—in a mental hospital, they would give him electric shock or drug him insensible, I knew that. At home, with Arthur, I was pretty sure whatever Arthur could see was wrong with him was more or less being ignored.

I had to be in Maine the next day—my alarm was set for 3:30—and there would be no time for me to stop and see him in the morning to make sure he made it through the night. I thought of leaving a note on his doorstep, but what would Arthur think? If he found it, would he even give it to Paul? All this was making me crazy. When I got in bed, I felt fear swarm inside me. I recognized it immediately: this is how Paul feels right now, I thought, and at the same time I was certain I could hear his footsteps coming down the path, could hear something going on in the garden, and I got up and looked out the window. If it was Paul, Gorm wouldn't bark. Jeff rolled over crankily.

"What the hell are you doing NOW?" he asked.

"I thought I heard something outside," I said. "Did you hear anything?" My heart was pounding.

"No, I was asleep," he said, in a growly voice.

I crept downstairs and went outside into the starless night and stood at the edge of the garden, where the soil was damp, but there wasn't anything there. I went back in, the steps cold under my feet. I slid the bolt to lock the porch door, which we never did, and then bolted the door to the house before going back to bed. It was a middle-of-the-night fearfulness that vanished by morning. When the alarm went off, I'd hardly slept.

When I got home from Maine, I went down to see Paul, but Arthur came to the door, opening it only half-way. I asked him how Paul was doing and he said, "He's a lot better, thank you. It must have been a bad cold." I

asked him if Paul remembered he had a doctor's appointment and he said yes, he had mentioned it. "I'm sure he'll
keep the appointment," he said, anxious, it seemed, to
close the door on the conversation.

The appointment was for 10:00, but when it got to be
9:30 I dialed Paul's number. He answered, in that small,
distant voice.

"Paul?" I said.

And he said, "I'm coming right up."

"Maybe it would be better if I came down to get
you," I said.

"No, I'll be there."

It was only a five-minute drive from his house to ours,
but it was another fifteen minutes before he got there,
dressed as if he were going to a funeral or a wedding: gray
slacks, light-blue dress shirt, dark-blue tie, dark-blue
jacket, and black wing-tip shoes. His eyes looked much
clearer than they had before and I was able to get a smile
out of him by telling him how nice he looked. But he had
forgotten, or had not had enough time, to shave or comb
his hair, which stuck up in three places.

When we got to Max's I let him off at the office,
giving his hand a little squeeze as he got out of the car, his
movements already mechanical. When I went back to pick
him up an hour later, it was fifteen minutes before he came
out the door, the robot I was beginning to recognize as
Paul. It seemed to take him a full minute to open the door,
walk through it and close it behind him, and when he finally reached the car I thought I felt the tension of anger
move into the seat next to me. He said nothing and his

hostility kept me from immediately plunging in. I drove out into the traffic. I had other errands to do. After about ten minutes I said, "So, how did you like Max?"

"Okay," he said.

There was a long silence before he came back with the information that Max had set up an appointment for him with another doctor in town at 2:30, one who might be able to prescribe something for his most immediate symptom, nervous tension. Max, being only a counselor, could not prescribe medications.

It was only a little past noon. "Want to drive up into Ashfield?" I asked.

"Okay," he said softly.

We drove along the winding roads, the sides lush-green with the summer, down as many dirt roads as I could find, and as we turned onto one, Paul looked into the backseat at Gorm, who I'd almost forgotten was there. She was panting anxiously. "I think Gorm wants to go for a walk."

I pulled over and we got out. Gorm tugged on the leash and set a quick pace down the narrow road. Grass was growing out of its center. No one came by, there were no houses in sight and I was glad—what would people think, I wondered, of this couple, the woman in jeans, hooded sweatshirt and jogging shoes, the man unshaven, dressed so formally, walking so stiffly, his face a black mask, the anxious dog on a leash leading the way.

We got to the doctor's office; I felt unsure, but went in with Paul anyway and sat in the waiting room next to him. He filled out their information and then came and sat back down next to me and together we stared at the wall in front of us, which was brightened by a poster: a big, colorful Hallmarkish picture of a rabbit with an irresistible look in his eyes. White letters over its head said: You're no bunny till some bunny loves you.

The nurse summoned patients one by one until she finally came to the door and said, "Paul Bolton?" When he got up and drifted to the door she held open, her eyes went up and down him and I thought she looked a little disgusted. Or was she frightened?

The doctor gave him a prescription for Mellaril, 10 mg., a "mood elevator," so we went to the drugstore. Paul was in there so long that by the time he got back in the car I had drifted off to sleep, listening to the radio.

When we got to the house, he went up to his truck and put his things on the seat and then came back and said, "Tell Jeff I'll be here for work tomorrow at quarter of seven."

I said, "Okay," and he drove away, gears grinding.

When Jeff came home I told him briefly what had happened. He pulled on the cold bottle of beer he'd taken from the fridge and said, "You shouldn't be doing all that, you know."

"Who else is going to do it?" I said, real frustration in my voice. "Arthur's not. Paul's not. *You're* not!" Jeff stood looking at me. "He said he'd be here at quarter of seven tomorrow."

"Yeah, if he's on time, maybe it'll be okay, but if he's late, it means he's still sick and I don't want him on the job.

In fact, I don't want him back at all. He's a fucking cripple."

The time came and went the next morning and Paul didn't come. Jeff left without a word, going too fast up the driveway, his tires chirping when they touched the pavement. About an hour later, Paul came up in his truck and, even though he could see that Jeff had already left, he parked and came in. He smiled and said, "I missed my ride?" I almost detected his sense of fun returning.

His eyes were clearer again. "How are you feeling this morning?" I asked.

"Better," he said. "I'll drive out to the job myself."

"Take it easy driving," I said, "the medication is kind of strong."

He was standing in the doorway and he said he would take it easy and without thinking I went over and put my arms around him and held him and said, "I don't want anything to happen to you, Paul." And he hugged me back, tight, and said, "It won't."

At work, I made phone calls. I called Max and I called Dr. Bennett and I called Arthur, and when I was through I was pretty shaken by what they'd told me.

Max told me that Paul had talked, though not in complete paragraphs. "He spoke volumes with his eyes, though," he said and I knew exactly what he meant by that. "What do you see in Paul?" he asked.

"I can't say exactly," I said. "It's something like hidden beauty, like there's something rich and unusual under the surface. I believe in him in the strongest way but I don't think I can tell you why. It's almost too complicated. It's a mysterious kind of attraction I have for him. It's almost like he's me."

There was a long pause and finally he said, "Edie, if you see something in Paul, I'm sure you're the only one who ever has or ever will." And then he said I'd better get Paul to a psychiatrist. "You'd better think about whether or not you want to take this on," he said.

"I already have, haven't I?"

He laughed. Max was round and balding with twinkly eyes behind rimless glasses. "It looks like it. In any case someone has to, because the biggest danger for Paul that I can see would be inaction. That would probably result in some pretty disastrous consequences."

I waited for him to tell me more specifically what they would be.

"Dr. Bennett called me right after Paul left his office and told me Paul was a 'fucking schizophrenic' and said he ought to be hospitalized immediately. I'm not into drugs or hospitals, except as a last resort—they're often the beginning of a whole other trip—so you better be careful who you take Paul to. I've got a name, if you want it. I've heard good things about him."

I took the name and called Dr. Bennett, who was much more abrupt, telling me simply that Paul needed to be hospitalized before putting me on to the secretary to schedule blood tests for the next day.

Then I called Paul, to tell him about the tests. I hoped

he wasn't home because it was Arthur I really wanted to talk to. Arthur answered, in his high-pitched nasal voice. "He's not home yet," he said when I asked. "Did he go to work with Jeff today?" He sounded concerned, which surprised me and calmed me somewhat. I said he had. "I think those pills helped, don't you?" I told him I thought they might be helping, but that there were other things that could help, too.

"He gets these spells, you know," he said, "then he comes out of them. We all get down, I guess," he concluded. "I really appreciate your looking after him like this."

"I care a lot about Paul, Arthur," I said and I searched my mind for something to add to that or justify it, but he filled my silence by saying, "I'll tell Paul you called."

I thought later I'd better deliver the message in person, which would give me a chance to see Paul's eyes. Their house was usually dark, but when I went down that evening I felt it was more so, forbidding and icy. Paul was there alone and he looked as bad as he had on Friday, his eyes dark-red circles of confusion and fear. It was only 6:30, the summer's light still strong outside, but inside the house was dark and extremely still. I chatted—How was work today? and all that, and How do you feel?—and I got OKs in reply. I told him about the blood tests, which Arthur hadn't mentioned, and I said, without asking, "I'll pick you up at seven-thirty tomorrow morning. Don't eat or drink anything after midnight."

I had brought him a box of chamomile tea, which I find helpful when I can't sleep, but I think by the time I left, after giving him a hug and feeling the damp heat come off his body like a furnace, it was finally dawning on me that herb teas are unfortunately not enough when you're dealing with demons.

When I got there the next morning, Arthur's truck was gone from the drive and Paul opened the door, his hair disheveled, dressed in his work greens, and I said, "Ready?" and he said, very slowly, "No, I'm not ready yet." And he went soundlessly up the stairs and I couldn't hear anything overhead where his room was, though I listened for the sounds of dressing, the drop of shoes, the opening of drawers and thought for a panicky moment, "What if he's sitting dumbstruck in his chair up there and I have to go get him?" But fifteen minutes later he reappeared down the stairs, dressed again so formally, and we went off to Northampton and his eyes again were set straight ahead, the lower lids caked with dried tears.

The blood tests didn't take long and afterward we stopped at the diner for breakfast. We sat in a booth and he ate a big platter of eggs and bacon and home fries but he said nothing. I took him home, and when I pulled up in front of the house he had the door open before I even stopped, and he got out without a word. I shut off the car. Every single thing I'd done I'd felt unsure of, yet I was in it so far there was no turning back. I followed him up onto the porch, where he had stopped and turned back toward me. "Paul," I said, taking him by the arms, "you have to tell me if I'm doing something wrong. Am I doing anything wrong?" He said no, but he looked down like a child ashamed and stood on one foot and then the other and kept his hand ever so lightly on the doorknob as I went into my spiel.

"Look, you have to make some choices. This is as far as I can go. The rest is up to you. You can go see a psychiatrist. You can check into a hospital. You can wait and see how you feel next week. You can tell me to quit, to leave you alone."

His answer was rapid. "I know I don't want the last one," he said, finally looking into my eyes.

"Paul, I can only do so much. I can make arrangements, maybe find a doctor for you, but I can't *be* you. You have to take it from there. You have to take responsibility for your life and you have to care what happens to you. You have to believe in all the possibilities that I see in there. You have to trust me to know that there's something very much worth saving. Having me believe in you isn't good enough. You have to believe it yourself."

"I believe . . ." he said, his voice still so faint, his eyes mirrors of pain.

"Which of those options do you want to choose? Tell me now while I wait." And he went into a dark cloud of silence I couldn't get through, only acknowledging what was outside him by constantly looking at the clock, a plastic wall clock in the shape of a teapot, dingy with cooking grease. Finally I said, "I have to go," and he moved toward me and hugged me. His embrace almost cut my breath off. "Come back after supper," he said. He followed me out, and when I got on the path I looked back and the image haunted me long after: Paul standing by the open screen

door looking after me, his face a twist of anxiety and blackness, still dressed so formally, only his necktie loosened.

When I got home I unplugged the phone and lay down
and kept falling into a sleep that my tension would ruin by
jerking me back to consciousness—my leg would jump or
my arm would hit out against the wall. I was groggy and
distant when Jeff came home. I wanted so much to talk
with someone about this. I got up off the couch and went
into the kitchen.

He pulled out a chair and sat down. He had taken the
metal box of dope off the top shelf of the pantry. He
opened the lid and dug out the papers, plucked one out like
a tiny Kleenex and pinched grass into a pile in the center
crease. He began to tighten it into a roll. "I've had it with
Paul. I'm taking him his tools tonight," he said, lighting the
joint.

I did what I could to sound calm and reasoning, but I
knew that that might be the end for Paul. "What difference
does it make? I mean, why bother? You never know, he
might snap out of this by next week. Give him another
chance." I tried to act casual.

He drew in a great breath of marijuana and held it so
that when he spoke, it sounded like he was coming up for
air. "Yeah," he said, "I guess you're right."

He stayed long enough to finish the joint and then left
again. I brushed my hair and got Gorm into the car and
went back down to Paul's. Arthur came to the door with a
broad grin on his face and whispered, "Paul's a lot better
tonight. I noticed it as soon as I came home this afternoon.

It's those pills," he went on conspiratorially, "they're the answer."

He went to the bottom of the stairs and called up to Paul and then said, "I've got to go out pretty quick to get a permit from Town Hall."

Paul came in and he did look a little better, but he still moved dreamily and he sat down at one end of the table and I sat at the other while Arthur sat in the chair against the wall. Arthur talked, cordially, as if he wanted to make me feel welcome, to fill in for Paul's silence. He asked me what Jeff was working on and had it stormed out where I was today and how's the dog? When the room fell silent, Arthur got up and said, "Gotta go," and he was out the door like a flash.

I turned to Paul, but he spoke before I did. "I went out for a ride this afternoon. I felt better when I got back. I thought about what you said and I think I'm going to be okay."

It was simple, what he'd said, and I can remember being skeptical, yet his eyes were clear and there was a certainty in his voice I hadn't heard in a long time. We chatted awhile and he did a lot to convince me that he was fine so I didn't stay.

3

The next time I went to see Max, even before I sat down he asked, "So first tell me what happened about Paul."

I summarized what had happened, finding it hard to express or explain parts of that most incredible week.

"You know, it's possible that you want Paul to change more than he wants to. Has he ever given you the idea that he wants to change? What has he done to make you think he wants to change?" he asked.

"I'm not sure I can answer that," I said. "It's certainly nothing he has ever said. It's more like some kind of overwhelming feeling that I have."

"I mean, if a guy is running a marathon and he falls

down and needs a drink, you give him a drink. But I don't get any sense that he's even in the race."

"Well," I said. I was getting angry. "He may not be in the kind of race you're thinking of. He's too different. But I think he does want to change."

"Okay," Max persisted, "tell me this. What's the difference between Paul and a Labrador retriever?"

"Look." The anger rose. "Paul's not some kind of dog I've befriended. That's really insulting. You really don't understand him. I'm not surprised about that. He's not easy to understand. It takes a lot of time and a lot of thought. Believe me, I've put both into him. He does come across as meek, but he's not a follower. He has a lot more strength than most of the people I know. The fact that he's in his own world right now doesn't make him weak."

Max fell silent and at last he said, "It might be that Paul is making you strong."

I phoned Paul that night and his voice was so small that I called back, thinking it was a bad connection, but he was still barely audible.

I asked him if he was still going to work with the Lion's Club at the Mountain Festival on Saturday. I thought I heard him say yes, so I said I wanted to come down and maybe we could talk. I did hear him say, "That sounds good." So I told him I'd be down after lunch.

I headed down to the mountain around one o'clock that Saturday. The weather had been oppressive all week.

The clouds were close to the hills in the distance and the laundry I'd done on Monday was still damp on the line. But no rain. It reminded me of Paul, the oppression, the heaviness.

The festival was crowded. There were pony rides and hayrides and clowns painting colorful circles on the faces of small children. Up on the deck of the main house, a band played a kind of sluggish Dixieland. I found the striped tent with the Lions' banner hanging from the tent poles. Inside, several men in aprons and chef's hats were flopping burgers and hot dogs on a portable gas grill and hustling sodas and paper plates heaped with food to the long line of customers. I had seen Paul's truck in the parking lot but at first I couldn't find him. Then there he was, kind of standing in the midst of the activity, eyes distant. He was not wearing an apron or a hat but instead had on a white Oxford shirt, sleeves rolled to the elbow, his gray pants and his wing-tip shoes. He spotted me and came over to the narrow counter.

"Want to take a break?" I asked.

He nodded and went over to one of the other men and said something and three heads turned toward me. We went up and sat on a grassy bank, away from the crowd, distant, but not out of reach of the toodling of the jazz band.

"I went to see Max yesterday," I said.

"What did he say?"

"He thought you should have a psychiatric evaluation."

"I've had that done already."

"When? When you were in the hospital?"

"Yes. They did everything."

I said, "Me too," and he swung around and looked at me.

"When I was a teenager nothing made too much sense to me, either. I spent some time on a ward with a lot of loonies and they did a lot of tests. I felt so distant from everyone, like I could never belong to anything or anyone. I felt totally alone. I heard voices, and sounds would get distorted into frightening, threatening noises. I couldn't stand to listen to the radio because the voices would come out distorted, as if they were taunting me."

While I made this confession, he was nodding, murmuring, "Yes, yes, I know what you mean. I had the same things, all the distortions."

"That's why I felt I sort of knew how you were feeling over the past week. I've always felt as if you and I had some sort of understanding, as if we knew this about each other."

Even before I could finish he said, "Yes, I've felt that too." I could feel energy coming from him. Light, *life* had come back into his eyes. It seemed the long silence had ended at last.

"Sometimes I feel like—kind of like a fake," he said.

"You mean, like you're a fraud, like this didn't really happen?"

"Yes."

I knew exactly what he meant—that the way people reacted to these feelings is out of proportion to how bad it really is, when in fact it was simply an unfolding of the real self. I said, "You mean, like maybe I was overreacting to all this, like it's not really so bad?"

"Going to all these doctors, it's almost a joke, they're not going to find anything wrong with me physically. They never have. This is just me. You're getting to know the real me." And I thought I read in his eyes: and it isn't all that acceptable, it never has been.

"The thing is, Paul, what happened to you when you were in high school, that doesn't have anything to do with the person you are now, any more than what happened to me has anything to do with me now. You don't have to be stuck there, but I think that you are, because all the people around you, your family and the people in this town, are mirrors for you, mirrors that are always remembering these things for you. A lot of times people in small towns peg you and then that's it. Small towns don't seem to know about evolution. They don't seem to know that people can change. And that makes it hard to change! I know a little bit about what I'm talking about. I'm not saying I'm where I want to be but I'm a lot closer than I was when I was in school. I mean, here I am, twelve psychiatrists later!" I said, spreading out my arms. I almost felt like laughing. He looked at me with surprise. "But there were plenty of times when it didn't seem worth it."

He had his knees pulled up to his chest, his arms wrapped around them. I put my hand on his arm, full of warmth. "It is possible to change," I said. "Did you ever see a hill where they've been mining? There's a copper mine up in Vermont, where I've just been, and it's such an illusion, to know that there's a mine inside that green,

green hill. I wondered how they knew there was copper in that hill and not in the other one beside it, just as green. The mine that they made inside is intricate, like a little city underground. Those men wouldn't have gone to all that trouble if they didn't believe that there was copper in there. They *believed* it was there. I believe in you. I can't say why. I just know that inside you is something very special, very wonderful.''

Paul rested his chin on his knees and looked out across the lawn at the busyness of the carnival all around us. I said, "I'll give you this guy's name, if you want to call him and go see him. It's up to you. I love you just the same, no matter what you decide."

He looked over at me, flooding me with his warmth. "I have trouble saying things like that, expressing how I feel about—people."

"How do you feel?"

"That's the trouble," he said. "I never felt about any-one the way I feel about you. I never felt this close to any-one, ever. But there's Jeff. Working with him has been the best thing that ever happened to me. I know that. How can I give that up? And for what? You're still married to him."

I wanted to tell him things would work out, but it seemed so complicated, a maze I could never exit.

He hopped up onto the balls of his feet into a squat, and put his hands together as if in prayer. "Let's go for a walk," he said. And we started up the mountain on the ski trails, made soft with wood chips. "Hemlock," he said, as we passed through the strong fragrance. He took my hand and we walked along in silence then, a long walk up the mountain and back down. When we got near the music and the people and the smell of burgers and fried onions, our hands broke loose. I said, "What do you think, are you going to be okay?"

He smiled down into my eyes with quiet assurance. "Yes, I think I'm going to be fine," he said.

And he was. This was not the last of Paul's "spells," as the family called them, but it was close. The "spells" did eventually vanish. I like to think that the reason is simple— that love came into his life.

My marriage to Jeff did end, finally, pretty much the way we had planned. The house that had taken us four years to build was finished and it was sold.

Paul helped me move. It was an hour's drive, one way, to the house where I would live temporarily, and in the truck, on the drive between the two houses, he talked, a long monologue, about us, about how close we had become, how much he would miss me, living so far away. It took several trips, making it a long day, and when we were done, he sat me down on the couch we'd just carried in and gently pushed me back, cradling me and kissing my forehead. He whispered, "I don't know why I'm telling you all these things today, but my grandmother always told me that if I ever felt this way about a girl then I should tell her, and Edie, I'm telling you I love you."

The day after Christmas, I wrote Paul a card so long it continued onto another piece of paper. I told him about the party I'd gone to on Christmas Eve, the gray-damp weather we'd been having. I told him all about my new puppy, Dune, a little clump of white fur small enough to hold in one hand, and how the now-old Gorm was adjusting to all this newness, especially the annoyance of this great surge of energy who pulled on her jowls until she snapped back. Then at the end I wrote, "There is so much left unsaid, Paul. I hope soon we'll have a chance to talk, to spend some time together."

We did see each other, anyway, while we worked on the house in Chesham, the house that was to be my home. I had been able to do some of the work myself, the smaller jobs. During the fall, I had taken some time off and worked out there alone, painting, caulking, raking, cleaning up. The house, off by itself deep in the middle of a wood of maples and oaks, had become a haven, a place where I could find peace. At times I was virtually lifted off the ground when I stood back and looked at that little white cottage all snug in the still woods. There was no one within miles, no signs of life except for the busyness of the chipmunks and squirrels, the chatter of birds, yellow ones, red ones, and lots of red-headed woodpeckers.

I rebuilt the stone foundation from the long-gone barn next to the house, and dumped leaves and sawdust and all the composty sort of material I could find into it. It would be my garden. I plotted it out, marking where the rhubarb would go, and raked it over three times, readying it for planting the following spring. I bought, on sale at a local greenhouse, a hydrangea, a lilac bush and a climbing rose, the blooms deep red, and planted them in front of the old chicken shed. I often got so caught up in the work that

I forgot the time, forgot to stop for lunch. I even took the broom and swept down the rocks that had been left when they hauled away all the junk, which had been considerable—car parts and old appliances were strewn about the place as if it had once been a junkyard.

Work continued into the winter. In December, a couple of days after I sent the Christmas letter, Paul and Jeff were working in the basement, jacking floors. The floor in the living room had the roll of a good potato chip and they were trying to straighten it. I'd gone down to help. Paul and I were holding up the beam while Jeff gradually tightened the jack underneath. When Jeff went upstairs to cut a post to fit under the beam, Paul waited until the circular saw had screeched on upstairs before he whispered, "I got your letter." He took hold of my hand then, balancing the huge beam on his shoulder. "How are you doing? Are you doing okay?" He held my eyes with his. When Jeff started back down the ladder he let go. "I'll call you," he whispered as Jeff's foot hit the bottom rung.

The next night, he did. His voice was faint, squeaky over the wires. We chatted a little and he spoke reluctantly, as if he were holding something back until finally he said, "Do you want me to come up there right now? I will. Just let me know what you want."

It wasn't what I had in mind. It sounded tempting, to be with him, but the idea of him getting on his coat and hat and driving out in the late night the long hour to Dublin seemed extreme. "Are you serious?" I asked.

"Of course I'm serious. I'll be right up." I loved the

gentleness of his voice. Lately, it had held in it a wonderfully solid optimism.

"Great!" I said, but then I backed off, saying it was too late, the drive was too long, the roads maybe icy.

"Okay, what are you doing Friday night?" he asked.

Friday was New Year's Eve, an evening I'd been dreading. I'd been invited to two different parties, both of which sounded deadly. What fun to spend it with Paul. "Nothing," I answered.

"Well," he said, "let's do something. Let's start the year together. I'll come over after work. I don't have to be home until Saturday afternoon so we can really live it up."

"That sounds like fun," I said.

"Do you want to come to my mother's for New Year's dinner?" he continued, elaborating the plan. "My sister and her family will be there and you could meet my mother."

I had only ever met Arthur. After four years of imagining what his mother and brother and sisters were like, I got cold feet. I didn't want to meet them at a holiday dinner. "No," I said, "I've got work to do. But that would be nice some other time."

He said he would bring a bottle of Yukon Jack, a sticky-sweet kind of whiskey that he enjoyed on rare occasions, and urged me to think of something fun to do. That was limited. After ten years of marriage, I was as unaccustomed to dating as he was. After all the time we'd spent together, it felt odd to imagine going out with him somewhere. I thought of the movies or maybe a coffeehouse in

Peterborough where I'd heard there was going to be some good music. I thought about it a lot. I felt totally in love, like I hadn't felt, I thought, ever. Stay until Saturday noontime? That stopped me. I looked through the storage chests for single sheets for the couch in the living room, but then I wondered if, after all, he might not sleep with me.

It was dark outside when Paul drove in, his headlights panning through the picture window. The dogs gave him an excited welcome. "Happy New Year!" he heralded as he came in, taking off his rubbers and leaving them on the doormat. He took off his work jacket and his cap. There was a light film of sawdust on his work greens, even on the lenses of his glasses.

"Happy New Year!" I said into his shoulder as we hugged. "Did you just get off work?" I asked, stepping back, brushing some of the sawdust from his arms.

"Yah, we worked straight through today."

"Did you bring a change of clothes?" I asked.

"No," he said. "I guess I can't stay tonight." He stood looking at me, confusion flickering across his face. I felt a pang of disappointment.

"But supper?" I asked.

He grinned. "Oh, yes, I'll have supper."

"Well," I said, "I was thinking we were going to go out, so I don't have much in the house."

"That's okay," he said. "Let's go to the grocery store."

We drove to the A&P in Peterborough and poked through the aisles. "Do you like chicken livers?" he asked.

"One of my favorites," I said. It was true. "I've got some rice back at the house. And some onions."

"And salad," he said, and put a round head of iceberg lettuce and a cellophane package of light-orange tomatoes into the basket and we went to the checkout. "Wait," he said, and disappeared. He came back, grinning, with a box of Sara Lee frozen cupcakes and a pint of vanilla ice cream.

In the car he took my hand and held it between both of his and told me not to forget how special I was to him. "I don't know where I'd be now if it weren't for you," he said. "Probably locked up in some loony bin." He laughed gently.

I turned in the driveway and shut off the engine. "I'm kind of disappointed, Paul," I said. "Why didn't you bring clean clothes? You're all dirty from work."

He stammered, clearly uncomfortable. "I guess . . . I don't know. I figured we wouldn't go out anywhere, we'd just stay here, just us."

"You could still clean up, just for me," I pointed out. I paused, looking over at him. "Are you afraid?" I asked.

"No, I trust you, Edie," he said. "I've told you that a hundred times. I trust you." He stopped. The car was cooling off and the windows were steaming up. "I am a little afraid—of women, I guess. You know, I've never . . ." He broke off and then started up again. "I'm a little afraid of you, yes, I am a little." He turned to me. "But I want to get beyond that. I have faith in us."

It was getting colder by the minute. "Let's go inside," I said.

We went in and unpacked the groceries. I made eggnog and poured it into the glass cups I found in the cabinet. He drank it in three gulps, sitting in the big wooden rocker by the stove. He watched me work and then got up. "I can cook too, you know, Edie. I love to cook," he said. "Let's cook supper together."

He sliced the onions while I made salad dressing. I put rice on to simmer. While I fiddled with the flimsy dial on the old stove, he came up behind me and closed his arms around my waist. "Edie, this is our night. Don't be cross with me. I loved that letter that you wrote me. I've read it over a lot of times. I wrote you a letter back but then I never mailed it."

I turned around in his arms. "How come?" I asked.

"I don't know," he said and he leaned down and kissed me.

I pulled back and had to laugh. "Whoa! Where did you learn that?"

He smiled and kissed me again. As the rice turned to glue and the lettuce wilted on the counter, we lay on the couch and began to exchange a string of promises that didn't slow down as the night passed. I finally turned off the rice, a solid lump. "I need to get cleaned up," he said. He took my hand, "Come on." He led me into the bathroom.

Almost shamelessly he took off his work shirt and his pants and then his very gray and very dirty underwear. I put the stopper in the drain and ran warm water into the old tub. He stepped in and sank down. I took a washcloth from the closet and unwrapped the sweet-smelling lilac soap he had given me for Christmas. He sat hunched in the tub, his knees drawn to his chest, his head bent. I lathered up the washcloth and touched it to his shoulder. "Is that too hot?" I asked. "No," he said, "it's just right." And I began to scrub. I felt I was cleansing a man who was destitute, a man who had wandered the streets for years. His skin, except for his forearms and a *V* at his neck was as white as the tub. It was as soft and smooth as any I had ever felt. It seemed never to have been unclothed before. I brought a saucepan in from the kitchen and filled it with warm water. With my hand I tilted his head back and slowly poured the water over it, soaking his hair, which parted in long greasy strings. I soaped it three times with my shampoo, rinsing it with saucepan after saucepan of fresh warm water. "All clean?" I asked.

"Can you cut my hair a little? It needs a trim."

"I don't know what there is around here for scissors," I said, "but let's see."

He dried himself with a clean towel and put on his pants, leaving his shirt and underwear in a pile in the corner. I found a pair of shears in a drawer in the kitchen and held them up. "What do you think?"

"Let's try it," he said, and we put a folding chair under the light and he sat down. I hacked away at his long hair with the blunt scissors. It was fine, so clean I could hardly get hold of it. It was just beginning to look good when he pulled the towel off his shoulders and stood up and put his arms around me and walked me backward to my bed.

•   •   •

These are secrets. I tell them now only because of what happened. I can't imagine what else would ever have compelled me to part with them. But I see now that if I am to tell the story of Paul I can't do it without including these most delicate parts of our life together. At the time, though I was dizzy with love for him, I don't know how convinced I was that our love could ever work. I was not yet divorced and I knew perhaps too much about what I then perceived to be Paul's weaknesses. By that time, in fact, I knew just about everything there was to know about him. All the information was in and yet it made no difference. My intellect fought the idea. My heart fought back.

After that New Year's night, I had a series of dreams; it seems this went on for months. Most of them involved accidents—sliding into ravines off icy roads, being in the backseat of a car driven by a madman. The dreams were vivid and insistent and I took to writing them down when I woke up, carefully noting as many details as I could remember so that I could try to figure out what they were trying to tell me. At the time, I wasn't able to, though I struggled, but I read over those scribbles now and the message seems clear enough: I felt out of control, helpless in the face of a force greater than I and I can see now that that force was my love for Paul.

It was interesting that I was the one filled with doubts, the one who held back as Paul proceeded with confidence. Sometimes I doubted our love because it seemed so unlikely, and sometimes I imagined I was using Paul's wonderful warmth and trust just to get me through the difficult months that followed my separation—not so much from Jeff, but from the life we'd created on that New Hampshire hill, so far from what we'd known growing up. Yet when I expressed these doubts to Paul, he would say, "Trust me," or, even more often, he would squeeze my hand and say, simply, in a voice filled with passion, "*Believe,*" and I could have no argument with that word.

Certainly it was not easy, what we had ahead of us. I had to get divorced from Jeff, and Paul, in a sense, had to get divorced from him too.

Paul continued to work with Jeff. Paul was a loyal man and he knew the jobs that they had taken on depended on his being there. He didn't want to let Jeff down. At least at that time, mostly what they worked on was my house, which the people in town knew as "Bide-a-wee," and we took to calling it that too.

Since we had torn the house down to its frame, what we were doing was equivalent to building a new one, albeit small. We made no changes in its style—it was still a little old post-and-beam house and it still looked old, but everything was new, the six-over-eight windows, the wide-board door, the wainscoting in the living room and kitchen, the wide-board pine floors, the chimney made of water-struck bricks, even the blown-glass bull's-eye windows over the front door. I used to like to tell people that the only thing original in the whole house was the raised panel door to the bathroom and the old claw-foot tub.

While the men worked, I watched the snow pile up outside the living-room window of my temporary home in Dublin. As the weeks and months passed, I watched the snow melt and the lakes thaw and the trees begin to leaf out. The tension between me and Jeff decreased. We all tried to ignore the oddness of the situation. I felt grateful to Jeff for keeping his part of the bargain and greatly looked forward to moving into Bide-a-wee. He seemed to be continuing on into a new life and apparently was seeing someone. And the love between me and Paul grew stronger and stronger. We wanted to marry. We dreamed of the children we would have. If it was a boy, we would name him Arthur Henry, not because either of us particularly liked those names but because both our grandfathers were named Arthur Henry, a fact we had discovered very early in our friendship. Such serendipity was too good to pass up. And if it was a girl, she would be named Anginette. We knew of no one by that name, but when we researched the deed to Bide-a-wee, we found that the house and the land had once been owned by Arthur and Anginette Seaver, a beautiful name we both thought, and one that should be carried through from the land that would bear her. It would all come in good time, we said.

After I moved into Bide-a-wee, Paul spent most weekends with me, and sometimes during the week I would go down to Northfield and stay with him in his crowded room, sleeping together in his narrow bed. The situation went on that way. Paul was still working with Jeff. It was a kind of half-in and half-out situation that made me uncomfortable. The prospect of moving in with me, which we talked about, seemed like a hard transition for Paul, harder than it would be for me. Though this was the first house I ever owned alone, I had moved many times in my life. Paul had never moved from the house where he'd grown up. Such changes come more slowly.

In spite of myself, I grew impatient. One Friday he called and said he would only be able to come up for dinner, that he and Jeff were going to start work early Saturday. I hadn't bothered to dress, was still wearing my sweatpants and sweatshirt, both smeared with gardening dirt. I stood at my kitchen window watching him drive in, my arms crossed over my chest, rehearsing my lines. He got out and came to the back door carrying rhubarb like a bouquet, and a steak, big enough for a banquet, wrapped in butcher's paper, the price marked in black crayon. He said Hi, Edie, and looked at me through worried eyes. He put his offerings on the counter.

"Would you like something to drink?" I asked.

"Water? How about a glass of water," he said.

I ran the water until it got cold and filled a tumbler for him.

"Let's sit down, Paul. We need to talk."

"Yes, I guess we do," he said.

He went in and sat on the far end of the couch and I sat in the rocker. My voice was small when I started.

"Where are we headed? Are we headed anywhere? If we are, you've got to stop working with Jeff. You know you can work for yourself. You know that you've taught Jeff just about everything he knows about carpentry. You're the master, Paul. There are thousands of guys out there who don't have half the knowledge you do. I know there is a need for someone like you in this town. You've just got to try it."

He sat, not saying a word, his eyes on the floor.

At last he said, "I don't know what to say. I guess I keep working with him because I don't know how to tell him that I can't anymore."

"I know. It's hard. But you have to. There's no choice unless you want to give up what we have."

It was starting to get dark outside so I went over to the corner and turned on the light. Then I sat next to him. "Paul, it's a risk. My grandmother always used to tell me, don't let go of the orange in the one hand unless you've got an apple in the other. You've got the apple, Paul."

With his free hand he reached over and pulled me to him. "You're all that matters to me, Edie," he said. Tears had pooled inside his glasses where the lenses fit close to his cheeks.

"It's true for me, too, Paul, you know that."

"I never knew a woman could be so loving. No one has ever done for me what you've done for me. No one ever could."

By then I was crying too and we lay together, crying quietly. I took off the gold chain he'd given me in January and gave it back to him. "I want this back," I told him. "But don't give it back to me until you've talked to Jeff. Just remember how much I love you and I trust that you'll do this. You'll know when the time is right."

"I'll be back tomorrow night," he said, before we kissed and he drove away.

He came late, after seven, bringing with him a bunch of purple and white lilacs so big that he had to go back to the truck to carry the armloads separately. And in the back of the truck he had two cardboard boxes of hollyhocks, big mature plants, that he'd dug up from his mother's garden to transplant to mine. We went right to making a bed for them. They were wilted from the heat and from the ride. We mixed loam and manure and peat moss in the wheelbarrow and set them down into it. After we tamped them down and watered them, we grilled the steak he'd brought the night before over a fire we built inside a circle of rocks beside the stone wall. We sat in lawn chairs beside the flames and watched the sky grow dim, Dune and Gorm asleep on the ground beside us. The sky was big and dark and quiet overhead. "I told Jeff I can't work with him anymore," he said.

After it got too dark to see, we went inside and climbed the steep stairs to bed. Once again, we held each other and cried, tears making his cheeks wet, my cheeks wet, the pillow wet. "I just want everything to be right for us, Edie," is what he said. For a while we lay there without speaking. It had begun to rain, and we could hear it fall gently on the roof window above us. Paul's tears seemed endless—no teardrops, just a steady stream that flowed. I knew that he was saying good-bye to life as he had known it. "Can we read something from the Bible?" he asked.

When I had first left Jeff and was living in the house in Dublin, Paul had sometimes brought me small pamphlets of Bible stories. He said his grandmother had given them to him once, when he'd been feeling down, and he gave them to me then to comfort me, to give me strength in the same way. He also brought me a small rough wooden cross, made of cedar. He pressed it into my palm one night before he left. He was not a churchgoer, in fact he had never belonged to a church. When he was growing up, he would go with his mother to wherever it was she was playing the organ. That was all he'd had of church. He had a lot of Bibles, though, mostly small pocket-sized ones. I have no idea where he got them and I didn't realize how many he had until after he died. It seemed that wherever I went in an effort to clean out and organize his things, his bureau, his truck, his shop, his trunk of personal papers, a small Bible would turn up. I had not gone to church once, not even on Christmas, since I was in school. It certainly had not entered into my life with Jeff. I rummaged around in some unpacked boxes beside my desk. I rarely threw a book away and knew I had a Bible somewhere. I finally came up with a Bible that had been first my sister's and then mine when we were in college. I thumbed through it. Passages were underlined and here and there, notes were scrawled in the margin interpreting certain passages.

"What shall we read?" I asked.

"Just about anything would be okay," he said.

I looked in the front to see if there was one of those calendar listings that tell you what to read at certain times of the year. There wasn't but when I scanned the index, I stopped at Job. I knew enough to know this had something to do with hardships. "Let's read something from Job," I said and turned to it. We read about all that Job went through, the terrible, unbelievable trials and losses he endured. I gave a small laugh. "Hey, what we've got is nothing compared to this poor guy," I said, rubbing Paul's shoulders. He smiled, the tears still wetting his face.

"Let's go to church tomorrow, can we?" he suggested.

"Sure, good idea," I agreed. It seemed far-reaching. I couldn't have imagined doing such a thing with anyone else.

We got up the next morning just before the sun rose. Paul was out first thing, tending the hollyhocks, and then we began making beds to set the flowers I'd brought in boxes from my gardens at the old house. Iris and lilies, foxgloves, chives and sage, peppermint and rosemary, boxes of pachysandra my dad brought for me. Rhubarb, some from Paul's garden and some from mine. The blackflies were pretty strong after the night's soaking rain, but we kept on going about an hour at a time till we couldn't stand it. We'd take refuge inside, read the paper a while until Paul would say, "Let's try again." We'd put on bug spray and go back, and together decide where the lilies should go or put in another row of pachysandra.

Around nine o'clock we cleaned up and got dressed, trimming our nails and putting on sweet-smelling lotions. Paul had brought his one dress-up outfit: a pair of gray flannel slacks, a light-blue oxford shirt, a dark-blue blazer and a dark-blue tie with tiny yellow Model Ts printed on it. His wing-tip shoes, polished bright. All except the shoes had come to him as gifts, one Christmas or another. Whatever, he looked very handsome to me, all dressed up.

There are two churches in town and we thought we

had a choice, but it turned out that one minister served both the churches. We had seen the signs, both of them announcing Mary B. Upton as their minister. The white-steepled one in Chesham was where we went that morning. I had admired this church from the outside a number of years before—I had even stopped and taken a series of black-and-white photos of its classic white clapboard façade, the windows like enormous house windows, clear panes in the center and colored squares around the edge. We drove the two miles to the church. The sun was up strong by then and the light made everything green and alive. There were no cars in the parking lot, a half-moon of dirt opposite the church. We parked and crossed the road. Down it toward the church came two white-haired ladies, arm in arm, clutching leather purses. We went through the white double doors into the coolness of the vestibule. Paul tiptoed to the next set of double doors and peeked into the sanctuary. Organ music drifted out. "There's no one there," he whispered.

I drew my lips tight and clenched my teeth in mock horror. The two ladies we'd seen approaching entered. "Hello," they said at once. "Welcome to our church." There was no turning back now. We went in. Mary B. Upton was seated in something like a throne up by the altar. She had short white hair and wore heavily tinted glasses and a simple blue robe.

We settled into the last pew. Paul sat close to me and held my hand in both of his. The floor creaked each time someone came in and within fifteen minutes there was a scattered congregation—thirteen white heads, and Paul and Edie.

There was no choir or processional. On the hour, Mary Upton simply rose and began the service, saying several prayers before we all sang a hymn, a tune I wasn't familiar with, each note that came out ragged seeming to reverberate in the expanse. Paul sang better than I, his voice a sweet tenor.

When we finished, Mary Upton spoke familiarly, as if she were conversing with us, speaking directly and without notes and pausing occasionally to find the right word. She was stern-looking, but her voice had depth and emotion, and when she said "amen," it came out the full two syllables. Her sermon was based on a reading from a letter from Saint Paul in the first book of Corinthians, chapter thirteen, a letter that ends: "So, faith, hope, love abide, these three; but the greatest of these is love. . . ." I know now that this passage is a favorite for preachers and it comes up frequently during the calendar year. Surely in my young life, I must have heard it many times over, but I had been outside this ecclesiastical world for so long that the reading that morning seemed completely new to me. Certainly to me now, as I think back on it, the selection seemed simply God-sent.

Mary Upton gave many examples of why love never ends, how it continues after death, how it can make a homely person beautiful. She said it in a dozen different ways. Love never ends. Love never fails. In another part of the passage was this: "Love is patient and kind; love is not jealous or boastful; it is not arrogant or rude. Love does not insist on its own way; it is not irritable or resentful; it does not rejoice at wrong, but rejoices in the right. Love bears all things, believes all things, hopes all things, endures all things.''

As we sat there, I imagined Paul and I marrying in this church, Mary Upton assisting us in our vows, a cluster of our families on either side, gathered for the joyous event. "Love never ends," she said for the last time before her benediction, and Paul squeezed my hand tightly and I looked at the elderly folk all around us and wondered what her sermon had meant to them.

4

Paul didn't move in with me. Though he loved my house and loved to stay there, he still returned to his family's place at the end of each weekend. I see it now, that he had unfinished business with his family. Houses have always reflected, for me, the lives that go on in them. My own, which was becoming his, was more and more beginning to reflect the peace and freedom we both found in it. His family's house reflected his bondage to his family, and being there, for him, was an expression of the tangled, painful and seemingly unrequited loyalty he felt for them. He was not yet ready to turn his back on all he had invested there. He may still have believed his investment would pay off, that he could somehow bring his parents back together again and in that reunion find some of the love he had poured into them over the years come flowing back to him. But it wasn't to be. Ironically, his parents did get back together again, but on terms that excluded him. The house, once again, seemed to play a central role: his parents evidently decided that their new life should take place in a new house, one without a room for Paul. They put the old, once-beautiful place in Northfield where Paul still lived up for sale.

So ended Paul's tenure in his parents' home, one that had included so little happiness it stunned me to reflect on it, a life lived, for most of his early years, under the eaves of an unheated attic. So ended also his connection to an ideal that would never be realized. It was a sad ending, almost a betrayal. But in the context of our relationship, it was a release.

As had been the case throughout his life, Paul heard none of his family's news directly. It all came to him like rumors, whispered truths from neighborhood gossips. Somehow, he found out where their new house was. We went snooping to find it. We parked the truck a few blocks back and walked through the subdivision.

"Oh God, right next to the highway? With all that noise?" His voice was no more than a whisper. "Oh God, look at that roof. God," he said. And then he looked the other way. "God."

"Let's sit in the truck," I said and we walked back.

"It's still a mystery to me," he said.

He slid over across the seat and took me in his arms and held me and held me and when he pulled away far enough to kiss me, I could see tears in his eyes. By this time the cab of his truck was all steamed up, so we had curtains against the world that passed around us on the nearby highway and lived in the little houses that lined this narrow street, and we held each other for a long time.

Paul and I helped his parents move. We drove up to his mother's house. She lived on one of Northampton's shady, quiet streets. Her apartment was on the first floor of an old house and when we got there her car was parked in front and Arthur's truck, different from Paul's only in color, was backed up to the cement stoop. We parked on the side and I could feel Paul's unease, which, when he was around his family, he seemed to wear like a skin, up and over his whole being. He had seemed so relaxed all weekend. At one point we were lying on the bed late at night. The rain was beating hard against the window and the warmth from the stove had spread through the house, so the covers were unnecessary. He lay against me with a half smile on his face. His voice had that hypnotic quality. "I love it here, being here with you. I can just forget about all that other stuff," he had said, throwing his arm off to the side as if that gesture could erase it all.

The rain held off while we carted all his mother's belongings out and angled and re-angled them all into the two trucks for the best fit. When both were packed to the limit, Paul and Arthur tied canvases over the tops, roping them down, over, and through for a tight seal against the weather.

We got into the trucks, and with Elizabeth in the lead

in her blue car, Arthur next in his green truck and me and
Paul bringing up the rear, we went, caravan-style, through
the streets of Northampton and onto Route 91.

After we'd emptied the truck, Paul said, "Well,"
drawing the word out the way he would when he was
getting ready to leave. "I guess we'd better get going." We
were standing in the driveway next to his truck and his
parents both thanked us. Then Elizabeth went toward
Paul. "What are you doing tomorrow? Are you working?"

"No," he said, "we're not working. We're taking a
holiday."

"Could you come down and help us?" she persisted.

I felt terribly awkward. I knew they needed our help,
but I didn't want to give up our day off. As always, I wondered where Paul's brother was, where his sisters were. For
Paul, there didn't seem to be any question.

"No, I think we're busy," was all he said.

"Is there anything else we can do before we leave?" I
offered.

"Oh, no," Arthur said, "No, we're all set. You've
done enough. We thank you," he said, making a slight
bow.

We stood in the driveway like four strangers. I wished
them well, complimented them on their new house and
Paul and I climbed into his truck. I didn't hear Paul say
anything, but as we pulled out of the drive, Elizabeth and
Arthur walked back to the door. She went in and Arthur
turned and waved a big wave and Paul lifted his arm and held
up his hand and kept his eyes on Arthur until he went out of
view. I thought then: will they miss each other, all those

suppers, all those breakfasts, those tiny decisions of sharing a home? Paul said nothing. He took my hand in his and held on to it, not letting go even when he had to shift gears.

It was late when we left and we were tired, so rather than make the trip to New Hampshire we decided to stay over at the old house before going home the next morning. The place was rougher around the edges than usual. The living room was a kind of lineup of furniture his parents hadn't wanted to take with them. We pushed aside the pile of blankets and pillows and sat on the old couch in silence, surveying the emptied rooms. I noticed that I'd tracked in dirt on my sneakers and asked him where the broom was. He looked for it and found they'd taken it. "That was my broom," he said, kind of flatly. "I just bought that!"

It was late. We sat back down. "Are you hungry?" he asked.

"A little," I said, peering skeptically into the kitchen. The pantry shelves couldn't be called bare but they were picked over. Left was a can of cherries, a box of lawn fertilizer, some bug spray, and a giant box of Bisquik that had the design on it they haven't used in many years. "I guess I'll need to go shopping," Paul mused as we looked around the gutted kitchen. We scrounged for dinner and came up with some frozen broccoli and some pork scraps wrapped in aluminum foil and God knows how old. But most of the pots were gone and so Paul put the pork in the trash and said, "Let's go upstairs."

Upstairs, he discovered his mother had taken a table from him, leaving the contents of its drawer on his desk. He stood studying these things, saying nothing. Finally he said, "I'm the last one here. The only one left." He pulled me to him and we lay down on his bed. He held me against him and we stayed like that for some time.

The next Sunday was Easter. We had been going regularly to the little church in Chesham, listening to Mary Upton's sermons and feeling the warmth that came to us through the scattering of elderly parishioners. We knew their names and spoke with them when we ran into them in the store. Being part of this church made us feel part of the town. But there was more to it than that.

On Easter, Mary's church had two services, one at sunrise, outside, on a hilltop that overlooks the town, and the other, the traditional service, at eleven. We planned to go to the sunrise service.

When we got up at five in the morning, the sky was a sharp blue. It was April. The ice had left the lake and the grass on the hills was beginning to revive. But the thermometer that Paul had put up outside the bathroom window rested on 24 degrees. We dressed like winter, layering wool over wool. Over my regular sweater, I put on my heaviest sweater and dug out my sheepskin hat. Paul put on his tie and jacket, heavy woolen pants, and over all this, his red-and-black-checked jacket. We pulled on mittens and drove through the dawning light over to Johnny Johnson's, an old hillside farm at the edge of town. The field behind his house is a long steep stretch of a hayfield. Most of the hills that edge the town are tree-covered. Johnny's field is the only one that is open and it gives a clear view of the town, the lake and Mount Monadnock.

We parked on the road and started up. It's a good walk up to the top of the field, where Mary and her daughter and son-in-law (who played the organ at the church) had already gathered, along with a handful of others, bundled in wool coats. Mary was wearing woolen pants and lace-up moccasins, a belted wool jacket, a hand-knit scarf and a yellow woolen hat pulled down over her ears. She had hymnals and typed-up programs in a picnic basket at her feet. Bob, her son-in-law, was wearing a full-length down parka with the hood up, the drawstring knotted at his chin. He was warming a trumpet with his gloved hands.

The wind was sharp and the sun, bright in our eyes, was just coming up behind the brick mills and various steeples of the town. Mary waited for everyone to climb up the hill before beginning with a prayer. When the last one reached the top, there were about twenty of us, including quite a few who did not ordinarily come to church Sundays. When we had quieted, Bob played "Jesus Christ Is Risen Today" once through on the trumpet, cranky with the cold, before we all joined in, our voices and the clear tone of the trumpet moving down into town on the wind. Paul and I pressed close together and shared a hymnal. "Jesus Christ is risen today, Alleluia! / Our triumphant holy day, Alleluia! / Who did once, upon the cross, Alleluia! Suffer to redeem our loss, Alleluia!"

How many times had I sung this hymn? It didn't matter. The words struck me with a certain power that gave me chills which had nothing to do with that sharp wintry air. My mind rolled back across the past few years, remembering Paul as he had been when I first knew him, remembering my own dark months, when I knew that my marriage to Jeff could no longer hold, remembering the black mask of Paul's depression last summer, the wall whose door I couldn't find. In my mind's eye, I saw his room and thought of the table his mother had pulled out from under his makeshift desk, without a word. I heard him say, "Please don't feel sorry for me." Alleluia! I sang along with the others. Yes, I thought, *alleluia!*

Rather than a sermon, Mary had a message. She spoke of Jesus, the lowly carpenter, and of his life and how he must have been regarded by those who did not understand him. She read of how he washed the feet of his disciples and then described this selfless, soothing gesture, as one we might extend to those we love. As always, she spoke with great conviction, as if we were challenging her, questioning her, and this was her answer. She told the Easter story and as if for the first time I heard the message of rebirth, the promise of life after death. Making a *V* backlit by the rising sun, Mary held up her gloved hands to demonstrate how Christ had held out his to show the wounds of the nails in his palms. Paul was holding my hand and he squeezed it tight through our mittens.

The service was brief, but we sang three hymns, Bob's trumpet carrying us through them. They were hymns filled with the news of the resurrection, filled with unmistakable joy that even on this cold and wintry morning relayed the promise of the warm summer days to come and offered great hope for the new life ahead of us.

Part Two

5

_____

I wonder now how much of our lives are preordained and how much are random events, scattershot and without order until the storyteller takes over. How much is in the mind of the storyteller? I could never have remembered all this. A lot of what I've written here comes from letters I wrote and journal entries, notes to myself. It is amazing to me what happens when I organize these details, make them into this story. Our lives, all of our lives, are simply an accumulation of details and events and are all but senseless until this is done. And I believe that some lives, even if the details are put in order, remain a random assortment of oddities, like what we find when we empty our pockets at the end of the day—do those miscellaneous coins and gum wrappers and paperclips and pens truly have anything to do with one another? It was this accumulation of the details of Paul's life, as they fell into place, that awed me. Because to me they had not only order but purpose. And through the sorting of them I see that the mystery of his life was solved through his death. What would this story be if Paul were still alive, here with me? It would not be a story. I would never write it. I would be living it instead. And it would not be the same story, since his illness and his death were what extended him beyond what I thought I knew about him when he was alive, when we were together.

By the time we got married, though, I had mostly stopped writing. To me, the main reason I wrote about Paul, about us, was the mystery of it. Our wedding signified the resolution to this. Perhaps the mystery had not been solved, but my curiosity had died into it. I had become one with it. It is true, too, that I write to soothe myself, and, being married to Paul, I was soothed just in being beside him. So there was no need to write. I believe that we write more when we are in pain. We are driven to it. To write when we are enjoying ourselves is more difficult. Perhaps the question then is, what is the point?

When we married in the fall of 1984, the happiness was unbelievable to us. This couldn't be, could it? We wallowed in it. As we had wished, Mary Upton married us in the Chesham church on an autumn day much like the ones for which New England is famous. The trees on the hillsides were orange and red and yellow and the air was cool. Friends and family came from far away and the little church was just about filled. Paul's mother played the organ, though she didn't much like the old reed instrument, more like a parlor organ, and she let us know it. But she played it beautifully, as she was so capable of doing.

My parents came, graciously, perhaps *gratefully,* accepting this new chapter in my life. During much of my marriage to Jeff, our relationship had been strained and there had been long periods of silence between us. Jeff was often rude to them in their presence, and disparaging toward them in their absence. But they never interfered and rarely passed judgment, at least that I knew of. They didn't know the darker side of my marriage. But they knew something was wrong. They had tried to like Jeff. Though they rarely expressed it, my parents didn't understand or approve of our lifestyle, the unorthodox inconveniences of woodstoves, hand-pumped water and composting toilets. What was this all about, they wondered? By contrast, they had liked Paul immediately. Much later, my mother remembered the first time she met him. My parents had come to visit and Paul was working up on a roof. I had stopped and tried to introduce them in a kind of shout. Paul put aside his hammer, climbed down the ladder, took off his hat and held out his hand. "It's nice to meet you," he said, smiling warmly. My mother and my father were often confused by and sometimes even fearful of the "weird" (their word) ways of my generation. Paul's old-fashioned demeanor pleased them. Paul loved my parents, in his trusting way. Later, Paul and my father, an amateur woodworker, shared many projects as well as long talks on the telephone. They were alike, quiet, strong and easy-going. It was during my marriage to Paul, and, I believe, through him, that I at last came to understand my parents, and indeed to love them.

After the ceremony, we had a party in the old schoolhouse. The electrician who worked alongside Paul on many of his jobs came and played his fiddle, and by the end of the day everyone, the very youngest and the really pretty old, joined hands and danced in a circle to the infectious rhythm of that country sound.

Friends came from so far—my sister came from Washington state, my friend Ellen drove up from Pennsylvania, cousin George and his family were there from Massachusetts—and we saw them so rarely that they all came back to our tiny house and spent that night with us, bedrolls and sleeping bags covering the floor, and in the morning I made pancakes and we talked and talked and lingered over coffee. As the morning got old, I opened the door to let the dogs out and heard the cry of a loon and we all quickly grabbed our jackets and went off, following the cry, down the path to the lakes, to see if we could see the loon and in fact we did and stood beside the water and waited for each mournful cry to come and talked softly in between.

By then it was time for all of us to go and we packed up and climbed into our cars and went our separate ways.

Paul and I put backpacks and camping gear in the back of the Honda and drove to Maine, which is where we loved to go. We didn't camp. We ended up at an inn on an island off the coast. It was informal yet elegant. The only room they had with a view of the water had twin beds, but that didn't matter. We had slept in narrow beds before. Besides, there was afternoon tea served on trays in the living room and a man came to our room each morning with a cart filled with firewood for our fireplace, which we lit after supper, for the nights were cool. There was croquet on the lawn and a little sailboat we could use if we wanted to, but instead, during the day, every day, we packed a lunch in our cooler and went to the end of the island, where there was a brief stony beach and great whalebacks of rocks that rose out of the water. We climbed up there and lay on the rocks and talked, as the tide washed in gently toward us and then retreated. When we got home, when people asked us what we did we said we spent most of the days watching the tide come in and out. It was true and it suited us.

It was a boom time in New England, everyone was moving here from downcountry, buying old houses and fixing them up, so there was no shortage of work. Paul's first job on his own was for an architect who lived in the center of the village. From then on, just as I knew it would, his reputation spread by word of mouth. He never had to advertise or ask around for work. Everyone who discovered him acted as if they'd found buried treasure. "They don't make 'em like this anymore," one delighted retired psychiatrist told me, after he'd arranged to have Paul fix up his kitchen. Gradually Paul built his business, working out of an old railroad station down the road. The ticket office was still there, just as it had been when the trains came through, and the waiting room, with its pine wainscoting and two-holer, had not been changed either. In the freight room, which took up more than half the building, Paul set up his machinery, his saws and planer and joiner. He bought a pot-bellied stove and plugged it into the old chimney. I moved my desk and typewriter into the waiting room and began to write there. His business grew. Before long the phone calls were mostly for him, and he had more work than he could handle.

Our life revolved around our work at the station, which we called the depot, tending to the gardens at the little house and being out on the lakes, of which there are more than ten in this town. The hot weather came and the cool green lakes offered relief. My cousin George is a boat-builder, and he sold us a rowboat, small and sweet, painted white on the outside, the seats a dark gray. He brought it to us the hot Fourth of July weekend, and we all went out on Seaver Pond, the lake so close to our house. We rowed across to the far side and swam off a rock, the hot sun drying us almost as soon as we got out. That was the beginning of many almost daily excursions for me and Paul. Going out in the boat, piling the dogs into the middle and making them stay still, became a ritual for us, a way to wind down after work and be with each other again after the day apart, but more often we'd go out in the early morning, before the sun came up, before the heat grew strong. We felt it was our own place, that empty lake, and time on it a kind of meditation with which to begin the day.

There was a rock we called Blueberry Rock, on the far side of Seaver Pond. We called it that because it was a small island of stone, ringed with wild blueberry bushes that hung out over the water. On hot Sunday afternoons we would sometimes row there with a picnic, spread a towel on the great mound of granite and make love on the stone, certain of our privacy. We knew this was just between us and the loons.

Once, as a kind of lark, we brought fishing poles. We had no licenses and the rods were from Paul's boyhood, the reels taut with a thin film of rust. We dug worms in the garden and brought them to the rock in a coffee can, but we'd not thought to bring something to put the fish into. We hadn't imagined we'd catch anything. It remained a story we liked to tell anytime the subject of fishing came up, how we hardly got the hook into the water before a trout leapt to the bait and was snagged, how we rebaited the hook and threw it back and the same thing happened all over again. In less than ten minutes we had caught five good-sized trout, Paul furiously honing a pine branch into a fish rack, both of us laughing so hard it was hard to keep our hands steady. In absolute disbelief, we took these fat fish home and fried them in the black skillet. And never went fishing again. Our return to the rock was always for making love. In his hospital bed, Paul would sometimes smile a small smile and say, his voice soft and as always without guile, "Let's go out to Blueberry Rock, H."

"H." It was what we called each other. "H" was a derivative of "Honey Bear." I don't know which one of us took up with that endearment first or where it came from, but eventually we rarely used our names at all, and in fact rarely even used "Honey Bear." Instead, it was "H-Bear" or, more frequently, "Bear." And, ultimately, "H."

So much of that time, that first year of our marriage,

seemed like a dream, especially when we were rushing back and forth, the long hours between Chesham and Boston. And it seems even more dreamlike now, as I look back, trying to recall if it really could have been as wonderful as I imagine. But it was no illusion. More than once, friends told us, told me, that when Paul and I were in a room together, they felt love.

And yet aren't interrupted dreams unbearable? There are books that have been written about experiments done on people who are repeatedly awakened from pleasant dreams, and how they eventually go mad from it. This is how it is for me, now. To have been awakened in the middle of that dream, it is unbearable. Still.

I cannot say that the dream ended when the cancer was discovered. It was much more gradual than that. After all, it was just a small lump the size of the tip end of his pinky finger, emerging from the crease where his thigh ended and his stomach began. "What is this?" I asked, running my finger across it one night after we had finished making love. By that time we had been married almost two years. "I don't know," he said and I knew by the way he said it that he already knew it was there.

But when he went to the doctor, our GP in Keene, the doctor assured Paul that it "wasn't in the right place for cancer." To this day I wonder what he meant by that. He gave him a prescription for antibiotics, under the assumption it was an infection. And when the lump didn't respond, the doctor was so certain it was a simple infection he just had the medication increased and tried it all over again.

He finally decided Paul should have the lump removed, a minor surgical procedure that involved only a day in the hospital. The surgeon came directly out of the operation, still dressed in his paper slippers, the pale-blue mask hanging loose around his neck. I was waiting in the lobby, watching an April snowstorm cover the greening grass. Paul was still in recovery. This man's eyebrows were great upsweeps, like windblown grass, and they moved, up and down, as he told me that the tumor was malignant. "Please, if you will," he said, "don't tell Paul about this. I would like to tell him myself when I see him in my office next Tuesday."

So for five days I scurried about the house, bringing Paul trays of food, and trying to be offhand about what the doctor may have discovered while I kept the horrid secret to myself.

When we went together to the surgeon's office, Paul sat facing the doctor, his arms folded in his lap. He was wearing his red plaid flannel shirt and his jeans and he pulled the shirt up around his neck and kept his hand there, lightly holding the two ends of the collar together, as he listened to the word *cancer*. The doctor's explanations were vague and laden with unfamiliar terms. Paul stared into his eyes, saying nothing, as if he was waiting to hear more, as if he wanted to say, Yes, but what does that *mean*.

We had no idea what these simple words, delivered by that surgeon, would mean. In fact, no explanation would have been enough, no amount of words could have told us. It was like being sucked into some great machine that whirled and spun us through the months and years that followed. Perhaps the most significant part was that the doctors could not agree on a diagnosis. At first they named it Hodgkin's disease, and then lymphoma and then non-Hodgkin's lymphoma. As each new set of doctors and hospitals set forth their hypothesis, we listened and then went home to our books, looking up the new diagnosis and reading the prognosis for each as it came, setting us forth along a path that would be instantly erased as another diagnosis emerged. And it all happened slowly, layer upon layer, each layer vaguely promising to be the last.

None of it made any sense. If I wrote a lot about Paul when I first knew him, I wrote twice as much during the time he was sick. I wrote then not to solve a mystery but more as if the act of writing were a relief valve. After I visited him in the hospital, I would come home and write, the details spilling out like long prayers, prayers that asked always for the reasons why. I read these now. They are strangely free of emotion, my lens panning the full range of the hospital, not just Paul and his struggle, but everyone, including the roommates and the nurses. I became immersed in Paul's situation. I was stunned by it. It was like an emergency alarm that was never answered. We just went on and on waiting for the ambulance to come, waiting for the siren to be silent, for the emergency to end, which in a way, it never did.

The confusion over the diagnosis took us from the small local hospital to the cancer center at Dartmouth in search of expertise, and when they confused us further we continued on to Boston, to the Dana-Farber Cancer Institute, a research hospital connected with Harvard University. We felt confident that Dana-Farber was as much on the cutting edge as any cancer center in the world.

Though I don't remember all their names, I remember each of the doctors' faces as they spun out their theories to us. The little tumor was sliced and sliced and sliced again and examined under many microscopes. I began to wonder how many slices could be taken from such a small piece of flesh. In one absurd episode, the tumor was lost in the mail between Dartmouth and Boston. And then, after several days of calls to Federal Express and different departments at both hospitals, the recovery of it became an almost ridiculous *aha!*—the little tumor had been misplaced in the mailroom at Dana-Farber.

The results of the pathology were compared by computer with information around the world. Confusion continued. It was never resolved, even at the end. After months of testing, consensus decided that Paul had testicular cancer and that is for what he was treated during most of his disease, even though in the end it turned out to be the wrong diagnosis.

To come to this diagnosis, they felt they needed to remove one of Paul's testicles. Although the operation is a relatively simple procedure, and later in his disease Paul endured far greater medical trials, he still recalled this as perhaps the worst part of everything he had to go through.

In terms of the cancer, the operation proved nothing. In fact it was probably needless. A week after the surgery, the pathology report came back negative. Just the same, it did not dissuade the doctors from believing Paul had testicular cancer. They explained to us, in their confusing jargon, that the tumor had not shown up in the testicles but near them and the tissue was of the same cellular configuration. In spite of the nature of the diagnosis, testicular cancer is one of the most curable of all cancers—a 90 percent cure rate. What they told us gave us great hope. And we did need that. Perhaps it was worth it on that level. In the end, Paul died of metastatic melanoma, which, had we known of it from the beginning, would have been a far worse diagnosis to come to terms with. But up until four months before his death we believed, and apparently the doctors believed, he had testicular cancer.

I look back on this one operation as a watershed. It brought a tempest out of Paul and crystallized his strength, which gathered from there and carried him through the rest of his illness with grace. It was July of 1986, only four months after he'd received the initial diagnosis of cancer. At first I had been concerned because he showed no response to the fact that he had cancer. It was as if it didn't register.

Doctors are so little help with the emotional side of this disease. Very early on, before we went to Boston, I worried that Paul would fall into one of those black depressions he had experienced before we were married, and which I feared would immobilize him. During a conference with one of the first oncologists he was assigned to, I asked this man what we could do if such a thing happened. Paul sat up straight in his chair, looking directly at the doctor, who was anything but compassionate. When he had given us the initial diagnosis, he glanced at his watch twice and acted as if there were more important matters to get to. Paul never forgot this detail, mentioning it more than once. We were sitting in a small office. The doctor was tall and thin, and he sat with his long legs crossed, his slender hands folded on his knee. I asked him, "What about depression, how do you deal with depression in situations like this? Paul has been treated for depression in the past. What can we do if that comes up now?"

He leaned back in his chair and looked carefully at his fingernails and then looked up and said, rather slowly, "When you're facing death, it's entirely appropriate to be depressed."

We repeated this many times to friends, and every time those words seemed even more stunning. No one had said Paul was going to die. We had not even mentioned it to each other. And the doctor had said it so casually, as if both the dying and the depression were natural and unalarming. But perhaps worst of all was how little those words had to offer us. They offered neither hope nor help.

And yet, in spite of that cold assessment, Paul never did get depressed during his long illness. It was as if the struggle with the cancer changed him, transfigured him. Or was it the struggle with death? Or was it the strength of our love that carried him? I'll never know the answer. Perhaps it was his faith in God, although this never came up in any kind of Bible-beating way. He went to church, but, like a lot of churchgoers, his mind wandered during the sermons and he never lingered over the lessons or got into any theological discussions. His faith was much more organic, something that underlay everything else about him.

The operation loomed. We focused on what happens when a testicle is removed, how it might affect Paul. Certainly there are a lot of myths about this procedure. Perhaps our main concern was that it would make us unable to have children, our great hope. He had already had radiation in the groin area, which the doctors said wouldn't *necessarily* sterilize him. But we had worried about it. Now the doctors seemed uncertain about the effect of this operation, too. They said that technically it would still be possible for us to conceive, but that it would be a good idea to "make a deposit in a sperm bank." Even the terminology repelled us.

In fact, this perhaps rivaled the operation as the worst experience of Paul's illness. For it, we drove down to a small laboratory in a huge office building in Newton. I waited in the untidy office, reading a magazine while Paul was ushered down the hall. I had thought that perhaps we would go to a room together, but they said no, I couldn't accompany him. I still can't figure out the rationale there. He was gone over an hour and when he came back he was pale and there was anger in his face. He was almost speechless on the way home. "Trying to jerk off in that little closet . . ." he started out, and then stopped and said something about how they had all these stacks of dirty magazines around. He was mortified. His dignity, of which there was a considerable amount beneath an ordinary surface, had been seriously injured. After incredible effort, he told me, he had been able to satisfy the requirement.

At least it was done and over with. It was shortly before the operation, so we focused on that. A few days after our visit to Newton, however, a rather unpleasant-sounding woman called me at work. (Fortunately we put my work phone number down on the bio sheet for contact, since Paul was rarely around his phone during the day.) She identified herself as someone from the sperm bank and very forthrightly told me Paul's sperm "wasn't worth saving." The sperm count was "the lowest they had ever seen," she said. I've never known why she felt she had to be quite so explicit in delivering the news, but was grateful it had come to me so I could translate it more gently to Paul. Which I did, that night. There were a lot of possibilities, including one that the radiation had temporarily reduced his sperm count. But the reason didn't matter. For us, right then, it was a fact, and even if the count recovered at a later date, the operation might knock that possibility away anyhow. We suffered a great loss that night, burrowed into each other's arms.

Two days later Paul checked into the Peterborough hospital. It was two days before the Fourth of July weekend. The doctors in Boston had urged us to have the operation done locally, since it was neither difficult nor intricate. It is a small hospital, provincial on both sides of that word. After he checked in, I sat on a chair next to his bed and held his hand, a pose I would assume countless times over the next three years.

He seemed calm then. I thought about the night before. He had been up all night, talking nonstop. It seemed he was almost crazy with the sudden realization that he had cancer. He had yelled at me—*Paul, yelling,* it was unheard of—that I couldn't possibly know how he felt. *I* didn't have cancer. *He* did. "You haven't been through *anything*! You don't care *what* happens to me!" And so on. It had been devastating. All night long he grew harsher and harsher, angrier and angrier, more and more crazed over the stupidity of the doctors. Until that night he hadn't said a single word against any of them. And he *swore*. Paul *never* swore. I'd never even heard him say "damn." It was just not part of him. All this had been confusing to me. Though the onslaught was not pleasant, I found myself saying *good,* he is releasing that anger, *at last*. And I felt surely it would be curtailed by the operation, if nothing else the drugs alone would derail all this. I felt almost relieved that the operation was so near. I hoped it would be a kind of passage for him.

The nurses worked around him, giving him a shot of morphine and then putting in an IV and several unnamed shots before they finally shooed me off so they could shave him and get him onto the rolling bed. Out he came, his head lolling on the pillow, his eyes woozy. The nurse let me push him to the operating room where we kissed, squeezed each other's hands and I said, "Good luck, Bear."

I went back to the room to wait. I had brought plenty of work with me, another scene I would repeat so many times in the coming years. My mind wandered. What an ugly operation. How cruel. I felt drained from all the tension and uncertainty of the past four months. Again, I had no concept of what lay ahead and looking back on it now I don't know how we do manage to pace ourselves, because I remember feeling completely spent, as if I had no energy left to face the next round, though literally years of these scenes would lie ahead of me. I kept hearing all the different doctors' opinions and felt incapable of sorting them out. An hour and a half passed as I tried to process it all. It was pouring outside, the rain beating hard on the air conditioner that droned sadly in the window beside me. Dr. Caspian, in his green cap and scrubs, padded around the corner, his footsteps muffled by his protective paper slippers. He sat on the edge of Paul's bed and told me everything had gone as he had expected but that we wouldn't get the pathology report until the following Monday. He winked at me and said, "Everything is going to be fine. Paul was awake through the whole operation [they gave him a spinal, which numbs the lower part of the body but doesn't put you out] and we talked about doing over my kitchen. He seems happy and relieved that it's over."

It was another hour before Paul came back from the operating room, a little smile on his face. Again, I felt relief that his anger had been taken from him. He was still numb from the waist down, so no pain had settled in yet. I sat next to him and held his hand for hours, while he dozed in and out of the morphine; at nine o'clock they asked me to leave.

The next morning I called him at eight and he sounded tense. "I'm coming home today," he said flatly. I thought I heard the anger back in his voice.

I told him I didn't think it was a good idea. "That pain is so crippling, Paul," I said. I wanted him to stay at least another day. I admit I felt weary from it all. How could I calm his anger at the injustice of such a tragedy?

I was also concerned because, with the long weekend

coming up, his doctor would be away. I would feel better with him under a nurse's care. But he somehow convinced his doctor that he needed to come home, even though the swelling and discoloration were grotesque and the pain apparently excruciating. (I learned gradually that doctors need no real encouragement to release patients. They seem eager to send them home at the slightest suggestion.)

I went over at noon to pick him up, after he called twice more: *when* was I coming? On the way home he started right in where he'd left off the night before the operation, as if there had been no interruption in his consciousness. *Why* hadn't we had this done seven months ago (when we first found the tumor), *why* had we waited so long? When we got home he got into his jeans and T-shirt and said, "Let's go for a walk."

"Walk?" I said. "You're supposed to go to bed."

"The doctor told me I have to walk!" he yelled and limped weakly out the door, leaning on a beech branch he'd fashioned into a cane.

I followed him. "Far enough?" I asked as we crested the hill.

"Nope." He plodded on, pale as a fluorescent light. In all he walked a mile. And slept not at all that night, again staying up talking nonstop, his eyes bugged, his hands flying left and right to make his point, his voice permanently raised. And then he'd drop back into sobs, terrible uncontrollable sobs that shook the bed. "We'll never have a baby!" he said. "It's all I ever wanted!"

I was crying too. I was maybe equally horrified by

everything the past week had brought us, though he was right, I didn't really know what he was going through. At intervals, as the night went on, we read from the Bible. It was his suggestion: "Just let it fall open and read," he said, his voice softening only then. In between the tirades, we prayed and we sang, over and over, a gospel hymn we sometimes sang in church, "Blessed Assurance," a song that ends with the refrain, "This is my story, this is my song. Praising my Saviour all the day long!" And as I sang it, I kept thinking, this *is* our story, but *why*?

By morning I was exhausted, yearning for sleep, but Paul popped up out of bed at 3:30, the light just new in the sky. He dressed for another walk. "Are you coming?" he commanded. I argued weakly and then, seeing the wall of resistance, put on my clothes. Back out we went, around the lake, another mile. He leaned heavily on his cane with each step, the painful, determined stride of a desperate man. When we got home, he took down his pants to show me the affected area. "It's like I've been kicked by a horse," he said, the anger still strong in his voice. It was true. It was exactly what it looked like. His remaining testicle was huge and the color of the skin was deep red, like dried blood.

"I think something's wrong," I said. "Let's go to the hospital." He didn't object and the doctor on call confirmed that he was bleeding internally, a hematoma he called it, a word I was to become very familiar with in the coming months. I told the doctor about the walks and he shook his head.

"Go home and get into bed," he told Paul. "Lie flat.

Don't get up. Get a jug for a urinal. Have your wife bring you your meals, everything. *Don't move from the bed.*'' And he gave him a prescription for sleeping pills.

We returned home, but the siege continued. Paul simply could not or would not stay in bed. Up and down he surged, raging. I tried to fix foods that would calm— custards, eggs, yogurt—but he ate only in little bits, nothing really. I listened and tried to reason. He continued to rail at me—"This is *your* fault!"—until he stopped, abruptly, his face changing dramatically as if his words were at last coming back into his own ears.

"Wait," he said, confusion and disbelief in his voice. "*What is this?*" He sank back against the pillows, his face full of concentration. Then: "I'm calling Herb."

And he grabbed the phone from the shelf beside the bed and dialed Herb, the minister who had replaced Mary Upton when she retired the year before. Herb was about our age and had tried in his own way to befriend Paul, though they had little in common. Herb came right over, climbing up the steep stairs to our little bedroom and sitting on the edge of our bed. He talked to us, talked with Paul about the anger he was feeling, experiencing, *allowing* to surface. Two hours passed. Mostly, it was Paul who talked. He was eloquent in his anger, which basically said, "I don't want to die." It was the first time he had said it. For the first time since the start of this terrible odyssey, Paul faced his cancer, came out of denial and acknowledged not only his illness but his anger, not only at the cancer but at his mother, his father, his brother, everything that had oppressed him. Everyone. It was devastating for me to watch, but somehow when Herb got up to leave, I knew we were going to be all right.

After Herb left, we cried and cried for hours. Over and over Paul said, "I've had to struggle all my life and finally I have a life worth living, I finally have a reason to live, and *now* look what happens!"

It was the first and last time I heard him say that, and the only time I ever heard him lash out against his family. Paul wasn't fond of repeating himself. Once he said something, that was the only time it needed to be said. Yet all that he had said during that almost demonic siege, all of those questions, pointless as they seemed, had to be asked, thrown out, *heard*.

The following morning he woke as if from a bad dream, that wonderful bright smile on his face again at last. It was like renewing a friendship. "We're going to make it," he said. "I know we are going to be okay. I feel reborn. *Reborn!*"

In a sense, this was his conversion, not so much in a religious way, though there was that in it, but in a spiritual sense. It was a purification of his soul, a washing away of his doubt, a strengthening of his resolve, which would be tested over and over again, right up until the moment of his death, but never again would he sink into that abyss of doubt and self-hatred. If nothing else, the operation had brought him that, a considerable gift in terms of what lay ahead, which of course we had no way of knowing would be so hard, so very hard.

6

In the fall, the tumor in his groin grew back. "Can't they do anything right?" Paul said, on hearing the news. He was beginning to lose faith in the doctors. In addition, the peculiar and uncertain nature of his diagnosis was turning the whole experience into something more like a laboratory study. "*This*," his doctor said to us after the tumor was removed, "will likely give us a better diagnosis."

The doctors at Dana-Farber decided to radiate the groin area again, which would involve about twelve weeks of daily treatments. My cousin lives in Wellesley and is connected with the college there. She arranged for us to stay at the first of what turned out to be four different apartments on the Wellesley campus, apartments ordinarily used by faculty but which were vacant for small periods of time. For each, we paid the college a nominal rent and slipped in and out like gypsies, arriving with a box full of kitchen utensils, one pot and one frying pan, another box full of cooking staples—flour and sugar, ketchup and mustard, herbs and spices—a futon, a set of sheets and towels, two pillows, my portable computer, and one rocking chair. This became our portable home, ready to be lifted into the back of the car at a moment's notice.

Eventually these places became sad and lonely outposts for me, places where I waited out Paul's hospital stays, but where he himself rarely came. But that first apartment, which was in an older brick building and had a fireplace with an ornate mantelpiece, felt cozy and was kind of fun for us. The radiation wasn't too rigorous or painful and it took only an hour each morning. The rest of the day I worked at my computer while Paul slept off the exhaustion that overcame him as a result of the treatment.

It was November and December, Christmas season. The stores and trees around the town were lit up and there was a much more festive atmosphere than we were used to at home. After five, I'd shut down my computer. Paul would get up from his bed. We'd go out walking. The apartment was only a block from downtown and only a block from the campus, so we could walk, hand in hand, around the paths of the college and then into town, looking in the windows of the fancy stores. On our way back, as we got closer to the apartment, we'd scavenge sticks and branches from the roadside, carrying them back to use as kindling to light a fire in the fireplace. It didn't seem so bad, then. Paul was going to be cured, we were sure of that, and meanwhile this interlude in this rather sophisticated environment, so different from our home, felt almost like a holiday. My cousin and all her children were nearby, so we had family around us. And we had each other.

Being in the environment of the cancer clinic humbled us and made us feel fortunate that Paul's illness was so localized. We didn't have a clear idea of how things would turn out for him, but, for us, there was a great deal of hope.

I remember one incident particularly. It was Christmas Eve. Paul and I were in the waiting room of the Radiation Therapy Department. It seems as if in all the hospitals we visited, this department, along with nuclear medicine, was always down in the basement, and even though the walls and floors were carpeted and there were no windows anywhere anyway, it *felt* like a basement. Most people who came for treatment had someone along for support. There never seemed to be enough seats for those waiting, so the rooms were usually crowded and there was always an air of tension.

On that Christmas Eve it was jammed. We stood against the wall, leaning against each other for warmth and support. Paul had a particular doctor for the radiation therapy. He had so many I'm amazed I can remember this woman's name—Dr. Lamb. She was young and sweet and her gentleness seemed to smooth over a difficult time. As we stood there, Dr. Lamb came through the double doors, pushing someone in a wheelchair. It took me a while to figure that the person was a woman. She was bald, like an android, pale as milk, but I could see the fine skin on her face, and her delicate hands. She wore earrings. The back of her neck, the only skin not covered by her johnny, was a fiery red, burned from the radiation. She was probably our age, certainly not older. A young man stood beside her. He looked stricken, terrified, but the woman looked defiant, her pale-blue eyes locked in anger. Dr. Lamb bent to her level and told her she probably would not feel well that night, that she should expect to be sick, quite sick. Paul and I looked at each other. It all seemed worse because it was Christmas Eve. Tears came into my eyes and Paul put his arm around me.

We spent that night in Wellesley. Since Paul had radiation treatments scheduled for the day after Christmas, there was no point in returning home to Chesham. We had no tree or any decorations in that apartment, which was really just one big room. The only signs of Christmas there were the stockings we'd hung on the mantel, mostly because it was so much fun just to *have* a mantel. We had filled them with small, fun presents we'd found for each other at the interesting shops downtown. That Christmas Eve, we lay in bed, which was no more than a futon on the cold floor. The remains of our hearth fire had burned down to an orange glow. We talked about that angry, defiant woman in the wheelchair and wondered how she felt at that moment. I cried for her once more. Paul said, "We're lucky, H," and held me tight.

That was the periphery of cancer treatment; if you hover there, it *is* almost oddly reassuring, because there is so much all around you to remind you it could be much, much worse.

In early January, after Paul finished his radiation treatments, we returned home to get back to business, to return to our lives, feeling in a sense that we'd had a near miss, that we'd veered away from some crazy head-on collision and had to pull over to catch our breath, to reenact in our minds just how close it had been, to think of what really *could* have happened.

We had been assured that this would probably be the end of it, that Paul needed only to come in once a month, just a safeguard, for blood tests and X rays, occasional scans, and a brief chat with Jack, the young doctor who remained with him nearly to the end.

We had been so confident of his cure that in the fall we'd put money down toward the purchase of an old barn on the edge of town. We had been looking for a place to own rather than rent, to replace the rented shop at the depot. The rent there was going up, and Paul wanted to be out from under that kind of uncertainty. Besides, he was outgrowing the depot and this barn would give him plenty of space overhead to dry green lumber and to store miscellaneous leftover materials. It was affordable for us because it was in downright dangerous condition, the underpinnings rotted and the stone foundation crumbled so that the sills rested on almost nothing at all. But Paul had fixed many barns in worse shape and felt confident that it just needed some jacking, a new foundation and posts underneath for support. Buying the barn didn't seem like a chancy thing to do. We knew that Paul would recover.

I was fortunate in my work. Though I was on the staff of *Yankee* magazine—indeed, both of us were covered by their medical insurance—I kept my own hours. Their only concern was that I get the assignments in on time. I could work out of a suitcase if need be, which I did, blessing the invention of the laptop. I wrote many stories in hospital lounges and those empty Wellesley apartments. I was rarely seen in the magazine offices during those difficult times.

But for that first check up, we felt so confident that things were on course that I remained behind at my desk while Paul traveled to Boston alone. I hated not going, but this follow-up visit seemed so routine we were sure there was no reason for me to have to go. So he went in alone and I went to work at my computer at the depot. In the early afternoon I heard the car drive in, close to the building. Paul got out and came into my office. I knew something was wrong.

"How did it go?" I asked, a new feeling of dread creeping in.

"Not good, Bear," he said, coming over to me and putting his hands on my shoulders, gently rubbing the back of my neck.

I turned and looked up into his clear brown eyes, felt the force of his worry coming back at me.

"They found some spots on my lungs," he said.

Even though I'd never experienced cancer firsthand, I'd read a lot about it. Something inside me sank. It had spread. We knew that this meant chemotherapy. This had been explained to us numberless times by numberless doctors, some of whom actually told us that the progression of the disease might be to its advantage in terms of treatment, that they couldn't really get aggressive about it until it got worse. Well, there it was, a turn that began a long odyssey into the world of cancer treatments and cancer patients, an experience that absorbed me to the point where I seemed to take on the disease myself. But that didn't come until much later.

Maybe one of the oddest parts about Paul's disease was the fact that, throughout it all, he felt fine. The tumors were never painful and if they had not been near the surface they would undoubtedly have gone unnoticed for a much longer time. Only at the very end did he experience any real pain or discomfort from the actual disease. Throughout the nearly four years of his struggle with cancer, any pain or discomfort came to him as a result of the treatments or the surgery.

Even after they found the tumors in his lungs, the debate over the course of treatment continued. In their uncertainty, his doctors scheduled a long round of tests, an incredible assortment of tests, one of which required him to lie on a steel table for two hours with his hands raised above his head and another where radioactive fluids were injected between his *toes*. Throughout all this, the doctors argued, sometimes right in front of us, finally telling him to come with a packed suitcase, in case they eventually did determine that the tumors were at a stage where they could be treated. I watched him put the few items into his blue duffel bag—his toothbrush and a change of underwear, his Walkman with tapes of Bob & Ray and Garrison Keillor.

From the bookshelves in the living room he took down several books—a couple of novels and two collections by Aldo Leopold and Wendell Berry, and one I knew he'd already read several times, Donald Hall's *String Too Short to Be Saved.* From the table beside his bed he took his small Bible and tucked it into the front pocket of the bag. It didn't take very long to pack, and pretty soon we were on the road to Boston.

Dana-Farber Cancer Institute is different from other hospitals because it deals exclusively with cancer. It is off to the side of Boston, in what always seemed to me to be a little city of hospitals. There are probably five major hospitals within blocks. To be down there, even out on the street, is to be in the hospital. There is almost a sterilized air. Most everyone, it seems, wears a white coat or carries a stethoscope. Either that, or they are people who look sick or very much in need.

Even within this hospital quadrangle, Dana-Farber is not like the other hospitals. It is more like an office building, eighteen stories high and relatively narrow. Maybe it seems this way because only two of those floors are for patients, the rest are offices and laboratories. Up to that day we had only been on the first floor, where the examining rooms are, and in the basement, where the X-ray department is. In one of the examining rooms, which were small and well lit and very clean, Jack spelled out the reality of the chemotherapy treatments. Neither Paul nor I had any idea what they entailed.

Jack was young. His skin was soft-looking and fair and he had eyes like a doe. He had been to Harvard, which showed a little in the way he dressed. He wore soft-colored, pretty ties—salmon and rose and coffee—and sometimes pink argyle socks. His hands were fine, with fingers that were almost delicate, the nails perfect and the cuticles white. He had an ageless face, so it was hard for us to read just how young he was. A couple of years into Paul's treatments, he celebrated his thirtieth birthday. We had no idea he was *that* young. I remember Paul saying, "Jeez," when he heard it and not much else. Later he said to me, "It seems scary to have someone that young in charge of my life."

Maybe it was because Jack was so young that he had this upbeat attitude that alternately put Paul at ease and irritated him. "Hey, buddy, how's it going?" Jack would say, entering the little room where we would often wait for long periods, our ears tuned for the right footsteps (Jack usually wore hard-soled shoes, so the heels made a tapping sound, different from the soft soles of the other doctors), the rustling as he removed Paul's chart from the slot and paused to read it before pushing the door open and bursting to life with his talk.

His explanation of the chemo had been straightforward, and somehow his words made it sound easy and harmless. We had heard it before, from other doctors, as they attempted to map out what might lie ahead of us. But when Jack told us about it, it had been almost a year since the diagnosis and we had gotten to the point where we both felt hungry for some kind of treatment that not only offered hope but assured us of the reality of all this, which, because of the uncertainty, at times had become almost like fantasy, albeit the dark side of fantasy.

Jack sat on the swivel stool facing us. We sat in oak armchairs beside the examining table. Jack had the three-ring binder, with Paul's name spelled out in Magic Marker on the spine, open in front of him and he had taken his beeper off his belt and set it on top of the open page. He never buttoned his white coat, and it draped open as he leaned back against the wall, his hands clasped behind his head. I remember once or twice feeling angry that his charm and good looks, the warmth of the colors he wore, had the power to soothe me, when in fact such superficial things should hold no sway over what we were dealing with, which was none other than life and death.

That day, he came up out of his relaxed lean and pressed his elbows onto his knees as he spoke. "Other places might wait for those tumors to be bigger before starting these treatments. But we're usually more aggressive. The chemo we have in mind for you is intensive. It will make you very, very sick, but that's what chemo does. It's like life in reverse. We have to make you sick in order to make you well. It destroys a lot of the good in order to get rid of the bad. The protocol we'd use for you combines three drugs. They're strong, two of them are heavy metals and that alone will make you sick. You'll stay here for a week and they'll give you the drugs at night, with a lot of other drugs to make you sleep. Hopefully you'll sleep through the worst of the side effects. Then you go home and you can be home for two weeks before coming back for more."

I watched Paul's face, looking for a sign that he was afraid or that this represented a crossing of some bridge for him, but his face remained calm and his eyes reflected almost a sense of excitement, which I knew meant he felt great hope in what was being offered him, that after so much time and so much uncertainty, so many tests, something was going to *happen*.

Jack went on. "Some of my patients, the ones as young as you, actually go home in between treatments and go back to work. I have one carpenter who has worked the whole time. I'm not saying it's a piece of cake, but it's not all that bad, really it's not." Jack sat back on the stool and pulled up his pink socks.

"The whole thing should last about three months. Sometimes, though, it can get drawn out a little longer. The drugs knock out your white blood cell count and that means you don't have much resistance. You have to be on the lookout for fevers all the time. A lot of patients get sick just from being so vulnerable, and you can't get the chemo when you're too sick. Sometimes that will make the whole thing last longer."

Paul listened hard, his eyes looking steadily at Jack, his face calm, still with that look of readiness. "What are my chances after this?" he asked.

"There's a 90 percent cure rate on this one, Paul. Your chances are very good." In my head, I tried to make calculations. At the very first, they had told us this same figure, 90 percent chance of a cure. And yet the cancer had spread to his lungs. Why would the cure rate stay the same?

I didn't want to ask. I wanted so much to trust what Jack was telling us and for Paul to hold on to his faith as well.

Paul gave a small, confident laugh and closed his hands together, a kind of muted clap that he used to give when he was ready to get going on a job. "Let's do it," he said.

Jack looked as if he'd won over an accomplice.

"When do we start?" Paul asked.

"Let's do one more test," Jack offered. "We need to know for sure those tumors are there." He leaned back again, hands behind his head, pensive.

And so Paul had the final, definitive test done. Afterward, walking down the corridor of the clinic, we saw Jack coming toward us. He held up his hand in a wave that looked more like a salute and he said, "The tumors are there."

He seemed kind of wired, and he had a little smile on his face. He took his gold pen and pointed at Paul's shirt, just below the pocket. "There's one there." He moved the pen to another spot, below. "And one there." And then he moved it to the other side. "And one there, right below your heart. They aren't big"—he held up his pinky finger and measured it down to the first joint—"like that, about the size of jelly beans." We were to learn that tumors are most often made analogous to food—grapefruit, walnuts, apples. I preferred it when they compared them to gravel and fists. That was more accurate.

Jack seemed rushed and started to move past us. There was an air of excitement about him. And strictly from his clinical point of view, I could understand this. Paul's cancer clearly dumbfounded his doctors. They weren't able to categorize it. But now, with the clear delineation of these tumors, they could move ahead, try to work their cure. But we found Jack's attitude depressingly detached.

"I've got to see another patient," he said. "You can go over to admitting and find out what room you'll be in."

By this time he was walking backward as he talked. He gave Paul a big smile and put his thumb up in the air. "Cleared for takeoff!"

Paul's room was on the fourteenth floor, a typical room with two beds, both of them empty, the starched white sheets stretched tight across the high mattress. Paul, still in his red-and-black-checked lumber jacket and work boots, went over to the window and looked out. His life now was as far removed from the woods and the birdsongs as ever it could be. I felt this so strongly as I walked over to stand beside him. I thought of our train trip to New York City, so long ago. This was not the kind of sophistication I had intended. Below us were the rooftops of outer Boston, and here and there a tree, sprigged with the feathery green of early spring, opened out from between the roofs. He put his arm around me. "Look at the rain," he said. It had been raining for days, it seemed, and now the rain splattered against the glass as if it were being thrown. The excitement I saw in him the day Jack described the treatments had given way to quiet. He had been quiet on the drive down and would remain quiet throughout the treatments, the determined concentration of a man working on the task at hand. I was his helpmate in this. I took all my cues from him. If he wanted to talk, we talked. If he needed silence, I left him inside his world of thought. We slipped into these roles. It reminds me now of other work we did together. It was not joyless. We kept our sense of humor and occasionally allowed small, pleasant moments in, but overall our job was the cure. Our job was to heal Paul. It was a task we entered into in absolute unity and we weren't going to let up until it had been accomplished.

Paul went back over to the bed and undressed, hanging his clothes in the tiny slit of a closet, just big enough for a couple of shirts but not big enough for his duffel, which we stuffed under the bed. It was a very small room. He put on the johnny, which was white with little blue squiggles on it. It made him look thin and defenseless. He got into bed. I felt tension coming from him. We had read over the pamphlets they had given us, learning all the side effects, and had cross-referenced them in the books we'd bought. Severe nausea and vomiting were listed for all three of the drugs he would be given, as well as kidney damage, lung damage and hearing loss, plus a list three paragraphs long of other things, including, of course, losing his hair. "You're going to look like some wise old man when you're bald," I said.

He smoothed his rough hand across his brown hair, which fell straight down from his part and was tucked behind his ears. "Could be worse things," he said.

Pretty soon a nurse came in and started taking blood. I felt tears coming, so I said I was going to get something to drink from the cafeteria and I went out, the tears balancing on the edge of my eyelids, threatening to fall. I got on the elevator and it dropped down between the floors like the earth moving out from underneath me. I sat in the lobby for a while, trying to change my perspective a little. The morning newspapers were all around on the tables and they showed pictures of the severe spring floods—high waters surging through houses and breaking down bridges and people lined up passing sandbags toward a half-built wall of rain-drenched bags. There was a picture of a policeman in a boat, rowing down the main street of some flooded city. I thought about how the water—nature—gets its way, how much stronger it is than we are, how something as simple as spring runoff can ruin people's dreams, their homes. I went back upstairs.

When I got back, there was another guy in the room with Paul. He was sitting in the chair, but dressed in a johnny. "Hi," he said, "I'm Mike Sheehan." He wasn't any older than Paul and he had a nice face with light-colored eyes and brown skin and a good head of salt-and-pepper hair. He said he was from Providence and he talked like it. He looked as healthy as any ordinary guy in his thirties.

"What are you in for?" I asked. Paul was sitting cross-legged on his bed, the covers up around his waist. The tension seemed gone from him and he was regarding Mike with his warm and interested eyes.

"I've got colon cancer," Mike answered. "Going on five years now. I've had six operations and thirty-six radiation treatments. Two rounds of chemo. My hair's fallen out twice and grown back. Nothing much has worked, so they're going to try this new stuff." He gave a little laugh. "Said it worked on mice!"

I looked over at Paul. His eyes looked kind but worried. Mike turned to the table and picked up a folded piece of paper. "The consent form," he said, tossing it over to me. "Here, go ahead, read it."

I took it. It started out by saying that there was no known cure for his cancer and that there was no reason to believe that this treatment, which was interferon combined with tumor necrosis, would help him. It made it clear that Mike could die from the treatment alone. "They told me it might give me a stroke, just a little one," he said, kind of half-laughing again. "But the effects will wear off after a few hours. In fact, my doctor told me not to cancel any plans for the weekend." He sat in the chair, looking relaxed, ankle propped on his knee. I could easily see him, beer in hand, partying with a crowd of friends.

I read the consent form through. It was similar to the one Paul had signed, but the consequences were much more dire. My stomach rolled. I handed it back to him. "Wow," I said, "sounds like you're in for a rough ride. Sounds like both of you are in for a rough ride." I turned to Paul, who was quiet, listening. I thought they were so brave, like two men standing at the edge of a stormy sea, getting ready to go out in a little boat.

The nurse returned, pushing a pole with a blue box halfway up, bottles hung from a hook at the top. "Hello, Paul," she said. "Are you ready?" Paul turned his eyes toward her and nodded. It was the IV pump and the bottles of chemicals. I was sitting by the bed and I took his hand, which was almost dripping with sweat. It was ten o'clock, past time for me to go home. I hated to leave him. I was the only visitor left on the floor. The nurse didn't seem to mind. I could still hear the rain outside and thought about the drive home, dark pavement in front of me the whole way. "You better go, Bear," Paul said and moved his hand up to my shoulder.

"I'll miss you, Bear," I said. "I'll call first thing in the morning." And I asked the nurse, "How early can I call?"

She smiled, gave us a soothing look and said, "We're here all night."

I leaned over to hug Paul, sliding my arm behind his shoulders where I could feel the sheets damp from the sweat of his tension. "I love you, Bear," he said, kissing my neck.

I drove home to New Hampshire, where I knew the dogs were waiting for me. It was raining with the same intensity it had been for days and the windshield wipers whacked back and forth. Ordinarily it was a two-hour drive, but that night it took longer. The roads on the way home were dark and the gutters swollen with new rivers. As I got closer to home, several of the roads I usually took were closed and policemen in fluorescent raincoats directed me onto detours by waving flashlights in the darkness with an urgent kind of authority. They sent me onto roads I didn't know. I drove through streams that had come up over the road and sometimes through places where the pavement had been broken up and scattered by the force of the water, which seemed to come down off every hill and up out of the ground where it never had before.

At last I turned onto our road and then into our rough, rutted driveway, rolling slowly through the low spots that were brimming like small ponds. My headlights lit up our little house and the back lawn, where Dune and Gorm barked and strained against their tie-ups. I got out of the car and started up toward them. The lawn was like a swamp. My feet made a sucking sound as I walked. The two feet of snow we had left that morning had almost completely dissolved in the warm rain and a river was running down the back lawn and into the basement, which was quickly filling.

This had happened before. I remembered Paul coming out in the middle of the night a year ago when we heard the water trickling into the house through the stones of the foundation. I had watched him from the living-room window. He made an eerie figure, working by the light of the floodlights. But his trenches diverted the water effectively.

I went inside, trying to remember how he had made those trenches. I got my rain poncho from the hook by the back door and the flashlight from under the sink, and from the shed I selected a shovel from the line of different-sized shovels Paul kept hanging there. I went up beyond the stone wall and started to trench in a way that made sense to me, making a path so that the rain would flow off to the side, away from the house.

I stuck the shovel into the ground and pushed with

my foot. The ground was soft and surprisingly easy to move. I thought about Paul and Mike, who were by now off on their voyages. The names of the drugs that were dripping into Paul's veins kept coming into my head. For once the drug companies were honest and didn't give these drugs pretty names. They sound like what they are. *Cis*-platinum. Vinblastine. Bleomycin. I said them out loud. I raised my voice into the rain. They hissed and belched from my mouth. *Cis*-platinum. Vin*blast*ine. *Bleo*mycin. They were like curses. And yet they were what were supposed to kill the cancer cells. They were supposed to be *blessings*. I couldn't think of them that way. The words kept coming, pounding inside my head in a crazy rhythm as I shoveled the rain-soaked soil and banked up the earth in dams made of stones and last year's fallen leaves.

During those first intense weeks of treatment, Paul almost disappeared from me. His quietness became a fierce inner concentration. I understood it and perhaps pulled into the same shell. If we were at war, and so many times I felt this was the right analogy, then being on the battlefield required that kind of concentration. There was too much going on, too many horrible scenes, one night after the other, to ever be able to sit back and reflect. It never felt safe enough for that. If nothing else, the world of Dana-Farber was an entirely new world, a new planet, inhabited only by those involved in this one singular struggle. Not just a struggle to stay alive. We are all involved in that. This was a struggle to survive what was meant to be the cure, an attack of incredible magnitude. I sank into it, a visitor in a foreign land.

Paul's work was always his salvation and this time was no exception. When he came back for his second round, he brought a portable drawing table and a variety of straight edges and sharpened pencils. Pushing past the waves of nausea, he would sit up in his bed, asking the nurses for extra pillows to support his back. The drawing table had small folding legs, meant to give the table a slant when set on a flat surface, but they were perfect to give the board stability in his lap. He spent hours leaning over his drawings, making plan after plan for this falling-down old barn. Working slowly and when he had the strength, he made exact diagrams of how the building would be jacked up, which end to lift first and where the jacks should be positioned, how it would be blocked, illustrating how the new foundation would be poured. He made sketches of his shop, which would displace a hayloft, and of my office, which would displace two box stalls and a tack area. This work totally absorbed him, though it pained me greatly. I couldn't imagine the work would ever get done, though it did and it is from that office, which is bright and warm and sound, that I write this now.

While Paul worked on his drawings, I became transfixed by everyone and everything around us. At first it was Mike Sheehan and his wife, Carla, a schoolteacher, who drew me in. Oddly, I looked at them as if they were going through something we were not. Mike was going to die.

That seemed clear. Paul was not going to die. That seemed clear, and that was the difference.

Carla Sheehan was young and pretty, and when she came to see Mike, which wasn't often, she had a look of terror in her eyes. I remember having the odd feeling that she was made of glass and that if our eyes met, she would break, so I usually looked away when she came to visit. Once I went into the lounge for a change of scene and she was sitting in there watching TV. I sat near her and she spoke to me for the first time. "What are Paul's chances?" she asked.

I told her about the 90 percent figure Jack had given us. "It sounds good," I said, trying to be upbeat, but then I gave in to doubt. I felt comfortable talking to Carla. "They really have never been sure of the diagnosis. His cancer doesn't follow the tracks exactly. It's not what they would call a textbook example. So there is some doubt." Carla listened closely. She said nothing, so I went on, "He's a mystery to them. Sometimes I feel that gives us more hope and sometimes I feel it gives us less. I suppose even when they are sure, it's a guessing game. What about Mike?"

She gave a small laugh and said, "Well, I know you read Mike's consent form. He knows he's being a guinea pig, but he figures if it can help someone who comes along later, it would be worth it." She looked back over at the TV. It was tuned to a soap opera and a very made-up woman and a bearded man were arguing in unconvincing tones. "It changes the way you look at things, the way you look at life," she went on. "One thing Mike can't stand now is to hear people complain. He hates it when people worry about things that don't matter."

I knew what she meant. Whenever I left the hospital, even just walking out onto the street or driving onto Route 9, I'd look at people, look in their eyes or watch them driving their cars, tuning the radio or smoking a cigarette, talking with their companion, whatever it was they were doing I used to watch them in awe and think: *They don't have cancer.* Their lives are traveling along well-mapped-out routes that have destinations. It was as if they had some kind of divine protection we'd been denied. And, yes, the things people talked about, the things that concerned them, suddenly did seem trivial and small.

That round ended a couple of days before Easter. Paul was pale and tired but excited to be going home. When I went to his room, he was dressed. His bag was packed and at his feet. He grinned.

"Ready?" he asked.

"Ready," I said.

He wanted to stop at the barn on the way home to check on the temporary posts he had put underneath in the late fall. He knew they were iffy. We had bought so late in the year that the frost was already in the ground. It is a big barn, three full stories and built as a hay barn, which is to say, not a great barn but a good one. It was sound, no rot. The problem was the underpinning, which was almost nonexistent. Underneath, the posts jutted out like bent knees where they had broken. Where foundation stones once joined the sills, now there was air. It seemed like a magician's trick—as far as I could see there was nothing whatsoever holding it up. "Habit," was Paul's half-joking explanation.

I hated it. I kept thinking that the barn was somehow symbolic of everything that had been happening: there was nothing supporting it and it was a miracle it hadn't fallen down. At night I dreamt over and over of that huge faded red building collapsing. I heard the noise of it in my head thundering down, over and over again.

Those temporary posts were all he had had time to do before his treatments had begun the previous fall. The day we stopped, on the way home from the hospital, it was mud season and everything seemed without solid ground, the earth beneath our feet as slick as Crisco. Paul fished in his pockets for the keys to the padlock that held the sliding doors secure. He popped the lock and pushed the doors open. It took a minute to focus into the darkness, but when I did I could see the floor plunged downward in a sickening curve. The floor had fallen.

We stood still, both of us staring silently into the dark barn.

Paul stepped forward through the door. In a moment I'd prefer to forget, I started to cry and shout at the same time. "Oh my God, oh my God, don't go in there! For God's sake don't go in there!"

He stepped backward and looked at me, uncertain, his eyes full of concern.

"I'm going to look underneath," he said and walked around to the back of the huge structure. Because it is set into a bank, from the back the structure looms even larger.

I followed him. I could see his pale scalp under his thinning hair, evidence the chemo was hard at work. His arms, usually puffed with muscle, were slender as a boy's.

Underneath, we could see the posts he had set last fall had dropped away. "The frost went out," he said. It was what he had feared. The main carrying beam sagged like a hammock, so low Paul could not stand up under it.

I cried out at him again. "There isn't anything you can do, Paul! You know there's nothing you can do! Not *now* you can't!"

In a crouch, he came out from under and together we stood back and looked at the sagging structure. Why hadn't the weighted beam snapped? I was crying like a child, "Christ, this isn't fair! It's not fair!" I shouted again and again.

When it comes to falling-down barns, there aren't that many who know how to fix them. That's why we'd gotten such a bargain on this one, because Paul knew how to fix what others could not. Or would not. There was only one person we could call, and that was Paul's father. "We've got to call Arthur," I said as we started toward home.

"I can handle it," Paul said. I knew he didn't want to call Arthur for a lot of reasons, pride being one of the biggest. It all seemed so crazy to me. It seemed to symbolize everything, this barn that wouldn't stay up but wouldn't fall down. It existed in some kind of crippled limbo and it so reminded me of everything else Paul was going through.

When we got home, I wanted to forget the barn. The daffodils were up all over, bright yellow splotches all around the still-brown earth. Right after I moved into the house, Paul had come over and helped me plant them. We bought a sack of 200 bulbs and we went around and found little places in the woods to plant clumps of them and we looked out each window and put them where we knew we could see them while we were lying in bed or washing the dishes. We weren't married then. I remember thinking, while I watched him dig a little hole and drop a papery bulb in, hey, this is the guy for me.

The next morning, Paul went out to the shed and gathered together his house jacks and some $4' \times 4'$ posts. I watched from the window as he loaded them into his truck. I was too scared to help him and I knew my fear might erode his confidence. He knew what he was doing. He understood as clearly as anyone on earth how a building went together and how it could come apart. Standing there, I prayed, and then, in a ridiculous panic, I thought, Christ, I would rather have a barn fall on him than have him die of cancer. It seemed so much more natural in the context of Paul.

Jacking a building is painstaking work. A half-turn of the screw each day slowly raises it, the movement barely perceptible. Every morning, Paul returned to the barn, crawled underneath the sagging beam and turned the screw. Gradually, day by day, quarter inch by quarter inch, he brought the floor back up to where it had been. It was only the beginning of how he saved the barn.

•   •   •

The treatments were roughed out as one week in the hospital and two weeks at home to recover before returning for another round. At first this schedule went along on course, but as the treatments intensified Paul became sicker. He would have his blood tested locally. If his fever rose and his white blood cell count dropped below a certain level, he had to return to Dana-Farber. Several times, this happened in the middle of the night. Once his resistance was so low he was put in isolation for three weeks. He had to wear a mask, and to visit him I had to wear a mask and a paper dress, paper slippers over my shoes.

To make the time pass more quickly, I used to read to him. Paul loved to laugh and he enjoyed Garrison Keillor's stories from Lake Woebegon. He had tapes of Keillor's radio shows that he used to listen to in his shop, before he got sick. He took the tapes to the hospital and often listened to them after I left at night. Paul was not Norwegian, but he identified with Keillor's characters—Clarence Bunsen and Daryl Tollerud. Keillor's new book, *Leaving Home,* had just come out, so I took that in and read him a chapter at a time, day after day. He loved the humor of these tales. In one section Keillor is telling of a Norwegian whose stoicism grows more outrageous with each incident. It had become something of a joke between us, how Paul downplayed his symptoms, how he always said, to me, or to the nurse, or to the doctor, "Fine," when any of us asked him how he was doing, even if he had just thrown up or was burning with fever. In the story, the man was experiencing what he thought was a heart attack. His wife says to him, "Are you feeling all right? Are you sick?" And Keillor goes on to explain: "He's Norwegian; he said, 'No. I'm just fine.' "

When I read this, the words muffled from behind my mask, Paul started to laugh.

I read on: "A Norwegian's dying words: 'I'm just fine.' On the field of battle, torn to a red pulp except for your mouth: 'I'm just fine.' Wreckage of a car, smashed to smithereens, a bloody hand reaches out the window and writes in the dust: 'O.K.' "

Paul and I dissolved in laughter, a laughter that reached far beyond the humor of this passage. Two nurses came running. They mistook our sounds perhaps for cries of help. Their faces looked alarmed. "What's wrong?" they asked. I realized then that I had never heard laughter in those hallways either. But they knew Paul, knew how ready he was to tell everyone that he was fine. So I read the passage to the nurses and we laughed all over again.

It wasn't that easy to find humor there. As Paul went back and forth between rounds, he had numerous roommates. Mike Sheehan turned up several more times and each time he looked sicker and sicker, but then so did Paul as the medication did its work. And eventually we lost touch. In the halls I saw the others, ravaged by their treatments. Bald, like space aliens or people in concentration camps, their faces smooth, no eyebrows, no beard, the eyes made bigger by the nakedness and the thinness. I remember one man, tethered to his IV, which was hanging from a pole like a coatrack on wheels, who walked around and around the hall, pushing his IV in front of him as he went. His head was pale and shiny and he had a look of anger on his face. The solution in the IV bottles was frothy from being pushed and pushed, shoved, really, all day long.

And of course there was the dying. During Paul's first week, the person in the next room was dying. The family, with red-rimmed eyes, holding rosaries in their hands as they paced the halls, was taking turns sleeping in the room on cots. Sometimes two or three of them would stand in front of the door to Paul's room, and they would hold on to each other and weep.

I especially remember when Belluscio died. He was the one with skin the color of iodine and bulging brown eyes. He was the one whose wife sat with him all day and whose family came at night, four or five of them crowding in the small space. He was, I had thought, about Paul's age, but I read in his obituary in the *Globe* the day after he died that he was only twenty-eight and an electrical contractor. That was hard for me to imagine. He was short and bloated to where I thought his skin would burst. He was sick all the time. It seemed every time I walked by his room he was coughing up into one of those little plastic kidney-shaped basins that are left in high stacks next to every bed. Every time I looked at him, he seemed on the point of death. Finally, they put him in a room by himself. When I saw him the next day, he was wearing an oxygen mask and his wife was sitting beside him, chewing her lip. He was turned toward her, his brown eyes bugged and sorrowful. They were holding hands.

About an hour later, I heard the sobbing. I was sitting next to Paul, who was sleeping. I looked out into the hallway and saw this enormous man—huge, a great, round face, a wide girth, his stubby hands emerging from his suit jacket. He was leaning on two other men, one of them a doctor. It was Belluscio's father. He was trying to say something but all that came out were great waves of sound. They walked him around and around the floor and he sobbed and sobbed. It truly seemed that he would fall to the floor if those two men didn't support him. I had never heard an expression of grief anything like it. I can still hear the soaring, almost operatic wails that came out of that enormous man.

About an hour later, I went by Belluscio's room on my way to the soda machine. The curtain around his bed had been pulled. Just his feet stuck out. When I went by on my way back, about a half hour later, the room had been stripped, even the mattress was gone, and soon after that his name was rubbed off the board at the nurse's station.

7

Was it inevitable that I would get cancer too? Some people think so. It was uterine cancer, and when I think of it I think of it as a cancer that grew out of Paul's, as if our bodies had melded together during that time, the cancer passing indiscriminately between us. If I was to survive, it was essential that I enact my own cure.

It was Christmas of 1987. By that time Paul had already endured an entire five-month course of treatment, only to find that the tumors in his lungs had been untouched by the chemicals that had so severely debilitated him. In July he had returned for another similar yet more intense round of treatment, with stronger chemicals added, compounds with even longer names, ones that promised more dire side effects. "The kitchen-sink treatment," one nurse casually dubbed it when Paul returned to Dana-Farber's fourteenth floor.

So it was nearly Christmas when these second-round treatments ended. Total body scans always follow the treatments, like exams at the end of a semester. We had driven to Boston on a slushy, cold morning, coming in before first light, ahead of the commuter traffic, breezing down Route 9 and then up the steep ramp into the parking lot at Dana-Farber. It was as if we were the only car on the road. Paul slept all the way. That was how he rode in the car then, the seat cranked back flat so that it always felt as if he were in a bed beside me as I drove. We had no idea what they would find when they did the scans. I don't remember that either of us felt great confidence that we would hear the tumors were gone. But neither did we expect to hear that they had again been left untouched by that incredible tour de force, that monstrous onslaught of toxicity.

Paul was extremely weak. He had lost his hair sooner and more quickly this time. One morning he woke up and it was on his pillow. He raked it together into a little pile, picked it up and dropped it onto his shiny head. It wafted away onto the floor. We both laughed at the absurdity of it.

His white blood cell count was very low, as it had often been during his treatments. Because of this, he had such low resistance that when he went outside he wore a mask, the blue paper masks they issued him whenever he left the hospital. I still have several boxes in the medicine closet.

He didn't need the mask inside the car, so he had

pushed it up onto his forehead, where it rested lightly as he slept. When we turned onto the ramp, he opened his eyes, as if that particular movement of the car signaled where we were. In the parking garage, he waited for me to come around and open the door. My footsteps echoed in the big empty space. He pulled the mask back down over his nose and mouth. I helped him crank the seat to the upright position. He put one foot out the door and then the other. I waited for him to find the strength to hoist himself up.

He had his cane, which he had sanded down and given several coats of varnish during a space when he felt particularly energetic. It was a handsome cane, showing the knots and gnarls of the tree branch it was made from. One of the most severe side effects he suffered from the chemo was the loss of feeling in his hands and feet. This, Jack explained to us, was probably from the heavy metals in the chemo, from the platinum. The way he explained it, I surmised it was a little like lead poisoning. But Jack kept saying he'd never known of a case so severe, he'd never seen it affect the feet like this. "But it's only temporary. The feeling will come back," he reassured Paul, again and again.

There was pain too, pain that went halfway up his legs. Paul, as always, played it down, saying "It's not so bad," but he would wake in the middle of the night and thrust his legs out from under the covers. "What's this?" I'd ask. "My legs. They hurt," he'd say. I knew it was bad, if he'd go so far as to say that. It was pain he couldn't hide when he walked. He leaned heavily on the cane and grimaced with each step. Three times he had fallen down the steep, ladderlike stairs in our little house, a terrible tumbling sound that left me momentarily frozen in fear until he'd say, yes, I'm okay.

Now, in the parking garage, he steadied the cane and then came up to standing. He was thinner then than ever, his jeans cinched in so that they fairly billowed out from the waist. He reached back into the car for his knitted hat, which he jammed down onto his head. "Okay, let's go, Bear," he said, through the mask. He was still inside that fierce, determined concentration, everything, everything had to do with the mission.

The tumors had been untouched by the treatments. Paul could hardly walk. He had sores on the inside of his mouth that stung and burned like open wounds. He had to stay to one side of the world, for fear it might contaminate him. He couldn't stand the smell of food. He had no hair, anywhere. His hands had no sense of feeling left in them. But the tumors continued to thrive in the dark unimaginable landscape of his lungs.

Jack sat in his usual place, on the stainless-steel stool, and we in ours, the Naugahyde armchairs beside the examining table. He delivered the news. "Surgery is really our only option now."

"I thought you told us surgery wasn't possible," I said.

"No, I never said that," Jack said. I couldn't believe what I was hearing.

"Yes, you did tell us that," Paul said, and our eyes met in disbelief. We had told many people that the reason for the chemo was because surgery was not an option. We had to have gotten that idea from somewhere. *We* certainly hadn't dreamed it up. We had been over this with Jack a year ago. I remembered it sharply, without question.

"Yes," I said, "you said the tumors were too close to his heart, that surgery would be too risky."

"No, the surgery is possible," Jack said, staring us down. "It *is* risky, very risky, but it's still possible. It made more sense to try the chemo first." He went on to tell us about the surgeon, an extraordinary man, he said, who had an incredible survival rate among his patients.

It's something I question now, whether or not this path was the right one, but I can only equate it to being locked onto a track, a downhill course like the luge, a path from which there is no exit, and one has to keep going. These were the options we were given and we took them.

We did, simultaneously, explore all kinds of alternative treatments. I think everyone reads about them or considers them in some way. I attended macrobiotic cooking school and we changed our diet substantially (although not that radically—Paul simply could not warm to seaweed). We ate whole grains and stopped eating red meat and drinking coffee or any caffeine at all. We ate fresh vegetables and fresh fruit and no refined sugars. It all made sense. It was something we ourselves could do, since most everything else seemed to be spinning wildly out of our control. But it wasn't enough. To turn away from the advice of these experts would have been virtually impossible. Many have done so. We could not.

By the end of the afternoon, we were sitting on the other side of the surgeon's desk. He was a big man with a heavy accent that was difficult to identify. We later learned he was German and had grown up in the Bronx. He didn't go into any detail about the operation and neither of us asked. He explained only that each lung would be operated on separately, the left lung first, where the tumors were the worst. "We'll wait a couple of months, wait for you to get strong again, and then we'll go after the right one," he said.

"How soon?" Paul asked. He and I sat numbly, side by side.

"We should do this as soon as we can," he said.

"Can it wait awhile?" Paul asked. "I have a garage I have to build." To the doctor, that probably sounded absurd, or maybe reckless, but I was beginning to feel we could make up our own timetable. We were so weary. Paul had been steadily under treatment for two and a half years.

Dr. Knoop looked at Paul with what I thought was a small measure of annoyance. He didn't know Paul as Jack did. That is to say, he had not come to understand him yet. "No," he said. "It cannot wait."

The X rays were clipped to a lighted panel behind him. They were the proof, and I kept looking at them, expecting, hoping to see the tumors. There were supposedly three or four on each lung. Dr. Knoop had shown us the dark spots, circling them with the end of his pen, but I couldn't really see them in the shadowy film. Everything looked gray and vague. I didn't know the code of the dark and the light of these pictures. I should have, by then, but maybe I didn't want to.

There was Christmas and then New Year's to get by.

Ten days or so. "Can you be here on January fifth?" he asked.

We said we would.

What else was going on then was the bleeding. I kept trying to ignore it. My period would come, a great, incredible flow that seemed to surge out of me with actual force. And it wouldn't end. The bleeding would wake me up at night. I would feel its warm stickiness all around me, staining through the sheets into the mattress. When I was driving, it would force me to pull over in search of a secluded place where I could squat and let the blood pump out onto the ground, leaving a mysterious crimson pool in the midst of quiet woods. No tampon or pad or combination of both was enough to stem it for more than half an hour. This went on for days and days. I was afraid to count them. It would subside and then return. It had been going on for months, mostly while Paul was hospitalized and I had not said much to him about it. How many concerns would we be able to hold?

I couldn't understand why this was happening. The mission was for Paul to get better. My own body would have to wait. Why couldn't it wait? I consciously tried to force back the blood. When I did think about it, though, I thought of this bleeding as a river of mourning for all the suffering Paul had endured and for the baby we would never have.

At last, I went to the doctor. This was maybe a day or two before the day Paul and I visited the surgeon. I went to

my doctor at home. He did a quick biopsy, a quick nip of
the uterus, a tiny pinch. And cheerfully said he'd call when
the results came in, but remember, there's Christmas now.
It probably won't be until the new year. Don't worry, he
said, you're fine.

We spent Christmas that year in the apartment in
Wellesley. We had brought a small tree from home and
propped it up in the corner, near the picture window. I'd
circled it with tiny white lights and necklaces of popcorn
and cranberries that I'd strung with needle and thread
while Paul slept on the couch beside me.

Being in Wellesley was the closest we could get to
being with family. A year had gone by and Paul's mother
and father had never visited him in the hospital. I occasionally called to fill them in on how he was doing, but their
responses were abrupt and, to me, inscrutable. They rarely
called. By now, of course, what with all my reading of
cancer books and talking with cancer patients and their
families, I knew all about denial and the other inexplicable
responses friends and family show to those with the disease.
And yet, I kept thinking, these are his *parents*. This was
their firstborn son. How could this be? Most Christmases,
we rode down to join them and the rest of the family for
what amounted to an annual get-together. But this year
Paul couldn't go to any family gatherings. Jack had advised
against it because of the possibility of infection. Besides, we
needed to be near the hospital. My own parents were in
New Jersey. They called almost every night and wished
they could be with us but it was too far, for either of us.

My cousin, who lived near the apartment, invited us for dinner. I could go and come back quickly, not leaving Paul alone for too long. Even so, I felt bad as I left him. "There's no point in both of us going without," he said, as I hugged him good-bye. "I won't be long, Bear," I said and stepped out into the December air.

It was a relatively mild Christmas, not much snow. I walked the short mile across campus, the earth hard under the thin soles of my Chinese cloth shoes. My cousin lives in a big Victorian house at the edge of the campus. On holidays, the house fairly throbs with activity. This day was no exception. The delicious smells met me while I was still on the sidewalk. It is a family that serves imaginative food, pâtés and sizzling cheese hors d'oeuvres, turkey stuffed with raisins and nuts, plum puddings and chocolate tortes. It was all there, coming out of ovens and off burners, piling up on the counters.

The feeling of Paul's absence was all around us. Almost without discussion, we loaded up two plates and then a third for my aunt, who helped me carry the hot plates back to the apartment. She was well, she said, thinking of Paul's lack of resistance, she couldn't remember the last time she'd had a cold. Paul pulled open the door when he saw us coming up the path. "Hi, Aunt Peg!" he greeted my aunt. "Merry Christmas!" His voice was soft and whispery and genuine. He was clearly delighted with our surprise. We had only three forks in the drawer and one of us had to sit on a suitcase, for we had just two chairs, but we quickly set up a holiday table and sat down to the feast before it got cold. Paul had not been eating much, but he ate and smiled and patted his stomach. He loved talking to Aunt Peg and so I let them get caught up.

A while later there was a tap on the front window. It was my cousin's little girl, Hayden. She waved merrily. Behind her, the rest of the children congregated, all of them waving to Paul. Naomi, Nathan, Jamie, Lindsley, Bailey, all bundled in snowsuits and parkas, their cheeks reddened by the cold and the excitement of the day. At various times, they had all been to the hospital to visit Paul, and now they had come to wish him "Merry Christmas," knowing he couldn't come outside. They danced for him, the cold air pumping out of them like steam from little engines. They blew giant multicolored bubbles up into the cold air. They put their arms against the glass and mimicked hugs and kisses. "We love you, Paul!" Hayden said, her voice muted behind the glass. Paul laughed and waved. It was a tender, good-hearted gesture of love and yet it unwittingly dramatized his seemingly never-ending isolation. There had been weeks and weeks of it in the hospital. He watched them dance. "God, I feel like the boy in the bubble," he said.

I don't remember that we talked about the surgery at all. The endless barrage of treatments had left us numb. This was simply the next step, and so far there had always been a next step. At various points during Paul's illness, I felt certain he would die. This was one of them. I had asked Jack over the phone what his chances were. "Well," he'd said slowly, "you'd better expect the worst."

The day after Christmas, we went to Maine. I was

working on a series of articles about land development in New England and wanted to take care of the last batch of interviews before Paul's surgery in January. I needed to go to the easternmost point on the coast, the city of Eastport. We had been there before together. It was actually one of our favorite places. Paul's eyes lit up when I suggested it. *"Great,"* he said. "Let's go!"

Before we left, Paul had his blood tested and the white blood cells had returned enough so he could dispense with the mask and move about in the world with reasonable caution. We packed our canvas duffel, which had become worn from its many trips in and out of Boston, stuck it in the back of the car and took off.

We hadn't been anywhere together in over a year. It was a long drive, eight hours in good weather, and the air outside was bitter cold. That didn't matter. It was as if we had left everything, the uncertainty of his surgery and my biopsy, in the driveway at home and driven away from it. We rode up like tourists, stopping in Camden to snap pictures of each other, hunched down in our jackets, with the harbor in the background. And stopping at Moody's Diner for a plate of homemade sausage and their apple pie, two of Paul's favorites, even though it wasn't time for lunch yet. In fact it was on this trip that he began to eat. And he began to relax. I could see the tension he had held in his face all year drain out, as if a plug had been pulled. An odd sense of peace came over him. I see it now in the pictures as I sort through them. There was a serenity about him, like an aura. It came out from him and touched me.

For music, we had brought Kate Wolf, and Paul

poked the tape into the stereo. She had died of leukemia in a Boston hospital several months earlier. A Boston radio station had played her music all day long in tribute, and after that we had loaded up on Kate Wolf tapes. Undoubtedly Paul felt a kinship with her, but aside from that, her music, a slow, serene stream of clear images, suited him. We started out across the causeway that leads into Eastport. We sang along with her: "Look at us sailing in, decks awash, but still afloat / And now the wind's come up / to rock us on the water. Riding out the storm like a ship safe at anchor. / Waiting out the long voyage, / 'round the Cape of Hope we'll take her."

We found a bed-and-breakfast run by a woman named Ruth. Her house was an old Cape Cod on a bluff overlooking the harbor, from which the wind blew cold and gray against the thin, rattly windows. We'd never met Ruth before, but she acted like she was some long-lost aunt who'd been waiting for our visit. Paul stayed in the house during the day, while I went about town doing my interviews. I'd come home at lunch and at night and find the two of them sitting together watching television, Ruth's cat curled contentedly in Paul's lap. Ruth knew he was sick, of course. She could see his frailty. She could see how hard it was for him to get up the stairs. He told her about the surgery one noontime, as the television danced in front of them. She pulled me aside that evening and asked me what it meant for him. I told her I didn't know. She looked frightened for him. At night she brought him extra blankets and in the morning she made special muffins for him.

We left Eastport in a blizzard. It was January 3 and we had to be back in Boston by the next day. We couldn't let the weather stop us. The snow was coming down hard. As we backed out of the driveway, Ruth stuck her head through the door. She still had her curlers in. "Come back again!" she called, putting her hand up. And then she called again, "Take care, Paul."

On the way out, passing along the ghostly streets of this ancient seaport, dusted now with the new snow, we saw an owl perched in a tree beside the bay. It swiveled its head and watched us pass, through the storm. Owls had haunted us ever since the beginning of this long, terrible time. Once, long ago, I'd seen an owl on my way to work. One of the women I worked with was part Indian, and when I told her about the owl, which had swooped down across the headlights of my car, picked up a rabbit in the road and flown off, she told me it meant that my life would change. Shortly after, I left that job and married Jeff. I had believed in the myth about the owl ever since. It always seemed to hold true. We had seen an owl just before Paul's first diagnosis, and at various times during his illness owls appeared, always before a turning point. Paul took my hand. "This is it, Bear," he said, "this operation is what's going to make the difference. We should have done it in the first place instead of messing around with all those chemicals. I could have been well already!" He turned and looked out at the snow that raced by the window as we sped out of town. "We've wasted a whole year. We can't waste any more time."

.   .   .

We used to joke that we could do a visitor's guide to all the hospitals in Boston, with a five-star rating of each cafeteria. So far, Paul had been a patient at four of them. "Instead of stars," Paul said, "we could use little meat loaves or scoops of mashed potatoes. Like a really good meal would get five meat loaves." As we drove in from Maine, we added New England Baptist Hospital to our list. It is on top of Mission Hill, a place where the wind seemed to blow all the time, especially during those cold, cold days of January.

Cousin George and my friend Jamie came in to be with us that night, the night before the surgery. If we had what we could call family in this, it was these two. George lived about two hours north of Boston and Jamie lived about two hours west and they both have families and children to hold them where they are. Nevertheless, they each found a way to be with us on numerous occasions when we needed extra support. This was one of them.

George came first. It was his birthday and I'd brought some birthday balloons and we had a card and a present for him. A birthday party seemed like a good way to pass this night. He took the chair beside the bed. Paul was in his johnny, sitting cross-legged on the bed.

Jamie came shortly after that, bearing a huge bouquet of flowers and a couple of presents. She's an artist, and after she'd set the flowers down beside the bed and given Paul a hug, she brought out a sheaf of papers. It was a giant cartoon she'd done of Paul. She'd done it in five panels. She taped the first panel to the wall at the end of his bed. It was a caricature of Paul, all the identifying characteristics in place—his nail apron draped around his waist, the Beaver Cleaver cap, the visor tipped up, the pencil behind his ear, the gap-toothed smile. A simple carpenter. The last image showed Paul, now evolved to Superman, with huge broad shoulders and tiny waist, a cape billowing out behind him. He stood beaming, his hands on his hips.

Paul smiled when he saw the final panel. "Naah," he said. He was calm, relaxed. Jamie beckoned me out to the hall. Whenever she had come to visit him, she would call me later and say, "God, he's like some guru. He just seems so *wise*, like he knows something we don't." Part of why she felt this was because of the way he looked, smooth and hairless, but much of it, I knew, was because of the way he looked out from within. He gave a feeling of inner strength to all of us. His roommates talked about it to me when he was not present. The nurses spoke of it. Outside his door, she showed me the other gift, which was a length of orange cotton cloth and a bright red lipstick.

I got the part about the cloth, which she had fashioned like a saffron robe, but I didn't get the lipstick. "What's that for?" I asked.

"You know," she said, "what's that dot that Hindus have in the middle of their forehead? The third eye?"

I knew what she meant and I started to laugh. "Oh my God," I said.

"Do you think he'll take it the right way?" she asked.

I hesitated. I didn't know if we should be clowning around *quite* this much. I felt it might be the last night I'd ever see Paul. But then I realized that this could well be the very best way he'd like to spend that last night.

"Oh," I said, "do it."

We went back in. "Okay," she said, "this would work best if we can get rid of the johnny."

Paul looked at me with mock confusion. "Go on," I said, "here," and I pulled loose the bow behind his neck and let the smock fall from his shoulders onto the bed, revealing his smooth, completely hairless body. Jamie and I wrapped the orange sarong around him in a way that seemed authentic. Jamie took the lipstick, held Paul's chin with one hand and tilted his face up. Between the space where he once had eyebrows, she drew a deep red circle. George was already laughing. "My God, I can't believe this!" I said. Paul joined us. "Wait a minute, wait a minute," George said. He took the bed controls and pushed one of the buttons. The mattress began to rise, lifting Paul above us. The illusion was complete. Our guru hovered overhead. And our guru was laughing, that wonderful uncomplicated laugh that came from deep within.

Timing onstage could not have been more perfect. Dr. Knoop strode in, big presence that he was. We all sobered, like children. He waited for the bed to be lowered. He looked around at us with an amused smile. "May I?" he asked, moving through us to examine Paul. It was time to think about what was going to happen in the morning.

Paul was scheduled to go to surgery at 6:00 A.M. The nurses said I could come as early as I wanted to the next morning. I came in at five. The corridors were quiet, the lights low. I turned the corner into his room; he was lying there with his eyes open. Warmth came into his face when he saw me.

"Hi, Bear," he said. I crawled in next to him, close to the welcoming warmth of his body. I gave him fast little kisses all around his cheek, down his neck and onto his chest. "Shoot," he said, "I'm just starting to feel better."

"Yeah," I said, "but you'll get better from this faster than from the chemo. It won't be so long. Are you scared?" I asked. He didn't act like it.

"No," he said, "just ready."

An orderly came in, pushing a gurney. My heart sank. "Bolton?" he said.

Paul nodded. "Okay," he said, and swept back the covers. Even though he still moved slowly, with the pain in his feet and the overall weakness, he hopped up onto that gurney with an air of confidence.

"Can I come too?" I asked the orderly.

"I guess so," he said.

I rode down with them on the big elevator, holding on to Paul's hand. The orderly rolled Paul into a small bare room. They brought me a chair and I sat down next to him. He was starting to feel drowsy from the medication they had given him earlier.

"I'd like to talk to my mom," he said. He lifted his head up and glanced around the bare room. "There's no phone here, is there?"

I went out and asked the nurse if it was possible to get a phone. She came back shortly with one, stretching the cord across the bare floor. I dialed their number and handed him the phone.

By that time it was a little past six. Arthur is always up by then.

"Hi, Dad," he said. There was a pause. "I'm getting ready to have an operation." His voice was gentle and unburdened by expectations. There was another pause and then he asked, "Where are you working today?" When they talked it was usually about the work they were doing. It seemed to be a plane where they understood each other. Finally he asked, "Is Mom there?" and then I heard him say, "Oh, okay, well, I'll see you." And he hung up.

"Mom was still in bed," he said.

"What? He couldn't wake her up?"

"I guess not," Paul said, shaking his head just a little.

I felt his hurt. I felt it as if it were my own. I picked up the phone. "Anyone else you want to call?" I asked.

He shook his head. I took the phone back out to the nurse and came back and took his hand. It was dry. "You aren't scared?" I asked again.

"No," he said, "I just want to get it over with."

He was getting more and more drowsy. When they came for him, he was almost asleep. I hugged him tight. "I love you, Bear," I said and watched them wheel him down the corridor.

Later, much later, he would recall for me that when he got into the operating room he heard the nurses doing their checklist of tools necessary for the operation. "I heard 'saw,' " he said, "and then I heard 'rib separator' and then I went under." I had no idea what it takes to get to the lungs. At that point, it was just as well.

The operation took six hours. I sat it out up in his room, walking, trying to read, lying on his bed napping.

There were times during Paul's illness when I had enacted great measures of faith. This was not one of them. I was expecting the worst, probably because I had been told to. Finally Dr. Knoop came in. I spun around anxiously. "He is doing fine," he said and sat down in the chair next to the bed. I sat on the edge of the bed.

"There were more tumors than we had thought," he said. They had operated on the left side first. It was the side with the biggest tumors and these were the tumors that were growing so near Paul's heart. It was the operation Jack had told us was not really possible, all of a year ago. "We took out maybe half the lung." It was then he explained the incision. He took the tip of his pen and began at my breast bone and traced an imaginary line around under my arm and under my shoulder blade and ended about at my spine. "We open that up, cut down through the ribs and spread them apart. That's the only way to get to the lung. When we're done we wire the ribs back together, but he'll have a lot of pain for a while."

"Can I see him?" I asked.

"No," he said. "He's in intensive care. You can see him in the morning. He should stay quiet overnight."

"What about the right lung?" I asked.

"Don't worry about the right lung," he said. "We'll do that in the spring, as soon as he's strong enough. There will be plenty of time for that."

"But won't the tumors grow by that time?"

"They are pretty small now." He patted my shoulder. "One step at a time."

I gathered my things and went back to Wellesley. I couldn't talk to him on the phone, I couldn't see him. I felt terribly disconnected.

In the morning I sped back down to the hospital and found my way to the intensive care unit. I had never been inside the ICU so I didn't know what to expect. I lifted the receiver beside the big metal doors and asked to see Paul. The nurse's voice came through the earpiece. She asked me to wait outside. I sat in the chair they had provided and restlessly flipped through outdated magazines for what seemed like an eternity. It was almost an hour before she came out. She led me to the far corner room, a room enclosed in glass. Even though I expected the worst, I never imagined this. The first thing I saw were his eyes, which looked out at me like those of a hurt animal, injured, suffering. He was barely conscious, but his eyes were filled with pain, as if he'd been betrayed. There was a lot of noise and an unbelievable network of obstruction between us. I couldn't possibly get near him. I waved to him stupidly. The entire bed was tilted almost upright. It was as if he were on display. Tubes almost as big around as garden hoses emerged from between his ribs and were attached to large glass jugs on the floor, jugs half filled with bloody waste. There was a tube coming out of his nose and his chest was wired to the heart monitor, which beeped rhythmically and flashed green lights. There were other tubes, other machines. Paul was breathing in short little gulps. The thing is, I was telling myself, is to look like everything is normal. Don't mirror alarm. I had probably read that somewhere. It was very much in my mind, yet I'm sure I was standing there looking numb and sick and scared. That is certainly the way I felt. Having been through all the months of wretchedness with him during chemo, I thought I'd seen it all. Not even close.

"Oh, Bear!" was all I could say.

In the meantime, my doctor had called and left a message on the machine at home. He wanted to see me in his office, as soon as I could arrange it. I knew that meant the biopsy hadn't come out well. On Paul's third day in ICU I drove back home to see Dr. Lilly.

The nurse ushered me into his office. I had been seeing him for years, but I'd never even been in his office before. I knew he had something important to tell me. "How's everything?" he said cheerfully as he swung into the room and settled behind his desk. He had no idea what was going on in my life.

"Okay," I said. I had grown impatient with doctors' chatter and wanted to ask if we could dispense with the small talk.

He went on with it anyway, something about what his wife had done that morning, making a joke out of it before he opened my file. "We have the results of the biopsy here and I have to tell you they aren't that good. Now, I don't like to have to use the word *cancer,* because people get kind of upset about that, but there is a *chance,* a strong chance, that this *could* be cancer. We feel . . ." He knew nothing about Paul.

When he said the word *cancer,* tears sprang out of my eyes. I felt myself spinning out of control. Dr. Lilly was not looking at me while he was delivering this report and didn't see my reaction until I snorted uncontrollably. He looked up at me. "Oh," he said, "wait, it's not . . ." It seemed as if he'd never encountered this reaction before. He began to search his desk for Kleenex. He had none in his office, so he got up and went out and came back with a box and set it down in front of me. He was kind of stammering, so I tried to tell him about Paul, about his being in the ICU right then. "Oh, my God," Dr. Lilly was clearly unhinged by this, in fact his distress helped me get myself together. He explained what needed to be done, a hysterectomy followed by radiation treatments, and then he said, "I know this is hard, but I think it ought to be done soon, as soon as your husband gets better."

I left and drove straight back to Boston. I was crying so hard I could hardly see the road. I howled into the emptiness of my car. I felt as if I was part of some kind of farce, some kind of sick sitcom where one misfortune piles on top of another until it is an absurdity of toppling fates. I wanted to tell no one, not because I wanted to keep it to myself, but because I was tired of delivering grave, bleak news. There was also a feeling that no one would believe me, that the depressing negativity of our lives would lose all credibility with this latest twist. And when, just exactly when, would I have time to have this operation? This was ridiculous, totally ridiculous. I thought of a story one of our neighbors had told us, before Paul's operation. He had said that his brother and his wife had gone together for routine checkups and the wife's X rays had revealed tumors on her lungs, so they did the surgery, just like Paul's, only to discover that they had confused the X rays and she did not have the tumors but her husband did, so he had to have the operation, right after. That would be worse, I thought, wouldn't it?

I waited to tell Paul, waited until he was out of ICU, waited until I could find the words. I might still be waiting except that he asked. I was sitting beside his bed and he still had several tubes coming from various places. "What did you hear about your biopsy?" he asked.

I wanted to invent something. I was so tired of grim news, of scary and dangerous medical excursions. "Not too good," I said and he closed his eyes. I knew he wanted to invent something too, some improbable, fantastical escape from this relentless wheel we were inside of.

"Cancer?" he whispered.

I nodded.

"Oh no," he said, still whispering. "Oh no."

I squeezed his hand. "It's okay, Bear. Just a hysterectomy. That's pretty routine."

"Oh, God," he said. His eyes were still closed and tears streamed from under his eyelids. Then he looked at me. "I don't want you to have to go through what I've been through."

If I had gone to him and closed my arms around him, if I had climbed into bed with him, if I had held him and rocked him, I would have caused him excruciating pain. Instead I held his hand tight and wept silently with him. "It'll be okay, it'll be okay," was all I could say.

Maybe this tip toward absurdity shifted the focus for

us enough to change the game. Maybe it took the emphasis off Paul, maybe it made him feel he wasn't so alone. If anything, it created an even stronger union between us. It might have even made it a little fun. I think of all of this now. None of it occurred to me then.

I found a doctor connected with Dana-Farber fast enough, and got a second opinion, which suggested the need to operate was more urgent than Dr. Lilly had suggested. Paul needed to be better first, all the doctors agreed about that. It was almost as if the doctors and the hospitals down there conspired to make this happen for us. I felt as if we were becoming a legend. Everywhere we went, the nurses seemed to know about us beforehand. "Oh, you're the two who . . ." they'd start out when we came into the office or the blood room or the radiology department.

Paul seemed to find this a new and maybe even better reason to get stronger faster. Dr. Knoop wanted him to walk a mile a day. He no longer used his cane. The feeling was coming back into his feet, gradually. It was cold and icy outside our house, so he took out a membership at the Y and every morning we'd show up there when they opened the doors at six and we'd walk around the running track, bucking the tide of early joggers as they bobbed around us. I still go to that track, never without seeing Paul, in his jeans and red-and-black-checked jacket, walking slowly and determinedly around that circle, his knitted hat set crooked on his bald head.

The most important thing was that he be strong enough to drive. They scheduled my operation for March 1, hoping Paul would be well enough to do that by then. His next operation was scheduled for April 1. This was close. It was probably going to take me six weeks to recover. It all seemed like familiar territory to me, like trying to squeeze an extra story into an already tough deadline. I'd done that before, I could do this. I think that's the way I was looking at it. To this day, I don't think I fully processed that operation. We had already faced the fact that we would not have children. That was beyond us already. Saving Paul's life was still our most important mission and this operation of mine simply felt like an encumbrance that had to be fitted between the two important things, which were Paul's lung surgeries. That was life and death. Mine was not. Or at least it didn't seem like it to me. It felt trivial compared with everything Paul had been through, and I somehow never felt concerned that I wouldn't survive this cancer.

I don't honestly remember very much about that operation. I couldn't get it out of my mind that I was being gutted. I kept thinking of the deer that hang from trees in the yards of hunters in our town in the late fall, their abdomens slit open and emptied. The analogy revolted me and yet it was all I could think of when I thought of what would happen to me.

In fact, almost everything that happened when I got to the hospital came to me through Paul's eyes. When they poked around the inside of my forearm, hunting for a vein for the IV, I thought only of Paul, and of how many times I'd watched the nurses run their forefingers down his arm, looking for a place for the needle. When they left me lying in a hallway for two hours, I could only think of how many times that had happened to Paul. When they fitted the cap over my hair as I was going into the operating room, when they had me count backward to go under, when I forced my eyes open into an arena made bleary by anesthesia and tried to tear the oxygen mask off, only to find I couldn't lift my arm—everything made me think of Paul, of how many times he'd experienced these things in the past three years.

There are only a few recollections that seem to have to do with me. I do remember being taken back to my room from the recovery room, where the sunlight was extraordinarily bright, and recall the surgeon leaning over me and speaking into my face, telling me that the cancer had not penetrated the lining of the uterus. "That's good news," he said. I remember the terrible pattern of the carpeting in the halls and how hard it was to push the IV pole alongside me when I went for walks up and down the corridor. And I remember the unmistakable sensation that went on for days, the sensation that there was a hole in the middle of my body, that there was literally a space where everything had been taken out. It was a very strong feeling and didn't really make sense to me. I imagined that if something is removed, all the other organs would settle back in together. Finally I mentioned it to the doctor. "It's like something's missing," I said.

"That's good," he said, "I mean, I *hope* something's missing." He laughed and walked out.

I see now how silly that must have sounded, but at the time I felt so frustrated that he didn't understand how incredible I found it that the center of me was *gone*.

·   ·   ·

I ended up spending a lot of time in that hospital. I kept getting infections. I got hepatitis. And, on one dreadful occasion, the incision burst open. Back and forth I went, in and out of the Boston hospital. Paul was still trying to get strong enough for his April operation, which was coming soon, too soon, it seemed. I felt as if I'd never be well enough. He stayed home, calling me often on the phone. For a long time, just moving his arms enough to shift gears was too painful. So was working the clutch with his feet. Gradually, he was able to drive into town for groceries or small errands, but making the drive to Boston was almost unthinkable.

There's a story that I like to tell when I am trying to describe Paul's extraordinary capacity for love. Having been through that major surgery, I kept thinking of Paul, what a desperate feeling it would be to recover from my own surgery only to face going through it all over again. I couldn't imagine, knowing the excruciating pain it had caused him, offering my ribs to the saw again, so soon.

It turned out that I would spend Easter in the hospital. Ever since our celebration of Easter sunrise on that wind-blown hilltop, Easter had always been our favorite holiday. Its messages of hope and rebirth spoke to us privately. We never talked of this, but the message of Easter had represented so much in our lives—I know that is why it meant so much to us. Of late, we had been unable to attend these meaningful services—instead we had spent holidays in hospitals, enduring the sad rituals (ornaments on the trays and decorations in the hallways) the staff performs in order to perk everyone up. But a hospital is indeed a dreary place to be on special days. They send all patients who can possibly go home, home, and a lot of the staff takes the day off. That particular Easter morning, I was lying on my bed, watching out the window. It was a wretched, slushy day. Cars edged slowly along the roads below. The floor was quiet. From my bed, I could look down the hall. It was almost empty, not the usual swarm of busyness. I felt sad and lonely.

Around noon, I spotted Paul coming down the hall. He no longer limped. His stride was almost back to normal. He was carrying an Easter lily so enormous it hid his face, but I could see his knitted hat above it and the arms of his red-and-black jacket encircling the pot. I suppose it is not out of the ordinary for someone to bring flowers to a loved one in the hospital, but these circumstances were not ordinary. I felt an overwhelming surge of joy. He set the lily on the table beside my bed. Its sweet perfume filled the room. He was smiling his broad, gap-toothed smile. He seemed genuinely happy to be there.

"Happy Easter, Bear," he said and bent to kiss me on the lips.

8

———————

Things happened very quickly after that. I think even then there was that feeling of swift movement, of the world spinning out beyond us.

Paul's second lung operation had been rescheduled for late April, by which time I had recovered well enough so that I could drive. Once again, he would be cut open from the breastbone, the incision passing under his arm and around to his shoulder blade, a cut that resembled the seam on a hardball. Once again his ribs would be sawed in half and spread open, a process that had been described to me as like hands pulling open the slats on Venetian blinds. Once again he would be wired and tubed together like some stuck animal. We knew what to expect. But this lung was supposedly the one less affected by the cancer, so we thought it might be a less severe operation.

It wasn't. As I sat there in Paul's room, waiting out the operation, it was an eerie rerun of the January scene. I had a growing sense of dread. The January operation had taken six hours, I remembered. Paul had now been gone for almost eight. Maybe the operation didn't get started on time, I thought. There were lots of reasons that it could be taking so much longer, but in my gut I feared it meant complications. When Dr. Knoop finally appeared, he sat on the bed beside me and softened the images of the tumors he'd removed from Paul's lung. The big one had grown to the size of an apple, he said. And there were many others. Small ones, which he likened to peppercorns, he had scraped off the tissue that remained. He'd taken almost the entire lung, he said. Weird images of the lung tissue loomed. Once, in a conversation with Jack about the possibility of surgery on the lungs, he had told us that if you took a lung and cut it open and stretched it out, it could cover the area of a regulation-size tennis court. He told us this so we would be sure to know just how elastic the lung is, how much of it can be removed without impairing its capacity. I'm not sure his analogy actually accomplished that, but the bizarre image remained in my mind. On hearing that Dr. Knoop had removed almost the whole lung, I thought of the other lung, seriously diminished. How far would Paul's lungs stretch now?

"He will recover quickly," Dr. Knoop said. "He is a strong man." He rose to his full and considerable height, gave my shoulder a squeeze and walked out silently on his crepe soles.

This time, Paul's days in intensive care went by swiftly, I hardly remember them, and soon he came home. It was May by then, and the days were longer and warmer. Since his first operation in January, we had been sleeping on the fold-out couch in the living room. It was easier for him not to have to climb the stairs. When he first came home, he often lay on the bed with the front door wide open, letting in the warm spring air. He could hear the birds as they worked in the trees all around the house. And chipmunks protesting along the stone walls. At Bide-a-wee, these were the only sounds, except for the occasional distant crunch of tires on gravel as a car passed by out on the road. Dune clung to us at these times. During our stays in Wellesley, the dogs stayed behind, cared for by my parents or our friend Jim. We were told that they brooded in our absence and waited anxiously, each time, for our return. Whenever we arrived home, they rewarded us with lavish displays of excitement and affection. Once, we pulled into the driveway and Dune, small and agile, whirled out of the back door and leapt into Paul's arms—such a perfect movement: it was like a ball homing into a glove. Gorm by then was fourteen, much more subdued yet forever loyal. But she was old, and finally, the previous November, when we returned from one of Paul's treatment sessions, we found her weak and listless, an anguished look in her brown eyes. Dr. Neally, our vet, diagnosed her with kidney failure and told us there was no hope. She kept

Gorm there at her office while we returned home. Gorm was our first connection, our Cupid. She had lived a good long life but nonetheless this was a wrenching loss for both of us. Paul went to his shop and made her a small pine box and we loaded it into the truck. We drove back to Dr. Neally's. Paul went inside. I stayed in the truck, crying uncontrollably. Dr. Neally gave the injection, while Paul held Gorm and stroked her forehead. He carried her back outside, wrapped in her green blanket and placed her in the box. We took her home and laid her to rest under the big oak tree behind the house.

That left us with Dune, who slept under our bed and accompanied us on walks, an important part of every day. As he had after all of his operations, Paul began to go for walks almost immediately. We would walk together. We both needed to gain strength and endurance. Walking the land around Bide-a-wee was a simple pleasure. The old town road, a path really, now used only by hikers and cross-country skiers in the winter, passed in front of the house and we would walk up it, Dune tugging us along on her leash, to the main road and on over to the lake, where we often paused to sit beside the water. Then we'd circle back down to where a rise in the road provided a broad view of Mount Monadnock. In the great universal sense, these were ours: the lake, the mountain and the woods, and we drank them in like a hot broth urging us both toward healing.

We always planted the garden on Memorial Day. It was our tradition. When that day came, Paul got out the tiller and together we worked the garden soil into a soft bed of dark loam. We had done this so many times together. We worked without talking. Long before we married, we had planted rows together. When he was done mixing the soil, he silenced the tiller and hauled it back to the shed. He took the hand cultivator from the hook on the wall and came back out to the garden. He was wearing his blue cap, the one that promoted Ford trucks, and his *Prairie Home Companion* T-shirt. This particular Memorial Day was warm. I held the cardboard box of seeds, and as Paul started over at the edge of the bed and scored a row, I followed, plunking the puckered green-pea seeds in a straight, evenly spaced line. When he got to the end of the row, Paul came back around and followed after me, closing the earth up over the new seeds with his hands. We started the whole process all over again with spinach. Then buttercrunch lettuce. I stopped and stood back to look at what we were doing. I couldn't believe it. It was only a month since he'd been in intensive care. He was still pale but he was stronger. Stronger and stronger. I went inside to get the camera and came back out to take pictures. We were planting our garden. It was 1988, two years since that first diagnosis on that snowy April afternoon. It seemed impossible that we could be doing something so completely normal, something so filled with hope as the expectation of a harvest.

A couple of nights before that, on a cool May evening while we were eating supper, we had been talking about the word *remission*. Of course we heard it all the time at the hospital. It had a kind of whispered status, as in *he's in remission,* sometimes uttered by the nurses. "But what does the word really mean?" Paul asked.

I went over to the bookcase by the stove, where we kept the dictionary for our Scrabble games, and ran my finger down to *remission:* "A state or period during which something (as symptoms) is remitted," I read out loud. We had a small fire going in the stove and it was warm where I stood. I looked up at him, over my glasses. He gave me his wise half-smile, which meant he needed more. I moved down to the next word, *remit,* and read the first definition: "To release from the guilt or penalty of sins."

I loved the way Paul laughed. It was full and easy. I can still hear the way he laughed at that, the way we laughed together. "Okay," I said, closing the book and wedging it back into its place, "we get the picture."

"Yah," said Paul, "sounds like a good place to be."

And it was a place where he found himself very soon after that. But I think actually that the proclamation that he was in remission came not from the doctor but from Paul, who had simply decided it in his mind. In June, we went in to Dana Farber for Paul's follow-up scans and blood tests. After all the tests had been completed, we were called into one of the examining rooms and Jack sat with us to tell us that the tests had shown no signs of cancer at all. Anywhere. I could hardly believe what I was hearing.

Paul sat up in his chair. His hair was coming back like the soft short fuzz of a young boy. He was gaining weight and was beginning to look like his old self. He put his hands together and rested his elbows on his knees and looked straight at Jack. "Then this means I'm in remission, doesn't it?" he asked.

I remember how Jack hesitated, a funny look in his eye that I didn't want to interpret. He answered Paul by saying, "Well, yes, I guess we could say that." I bit back the temptation to ask how else he might interpret it. I knew that for one thing there was very little else to offer after this, should there be a recurrence. In the earlier days, when Jack was so much more assuring about Paul's chances of recovery, when he still used the word "cure," he used to say to us, "As long as there is another step for us to offer you, then there's hope. It's when we run out of choices that you should start to worry." I knew in a sense that he had run out of options, but that he wasn't saying so. It was like a silent conspiracy. If we didn't ask, he didn't have to tell us. If the tumors came back again into the lungs, chemotherapy was no longer an option and there wasn't much left of the lungs to remove. It was a path I didn't want to follow in my mind. So I heard the word *remission* in the same loud way that Paul said it. *Remission.* Forget about that tentative look on Jack's face. Blot it out. *Remission.* It was all we wanted to hear.

Jack topped it off by telling us he didn't need to see Paul again until September. We had never gone more than a month without a trip to Boston, without the say-so of the X ray. I had been to my doctor for a checkup the week before. He, too, had scheduled my next appointment for September. This gave us an unbelievable sense of release, of freedom. A sense even of victory. We left Dana-Farber giddy. We walked down to the Coop and bought Tracy

Chapman's new tape. On the way home in the car we played it turned up loud as we sped north along Route 128, both of us singing, singing hard and loud, especially the verses about freedom, and laughing in between. When the tape ended, he popped it out and turned to me, leaning over to look into my eyes.

"Is this really true?" he asked.

"I don't know," I said, "but I don't dare question it. Let's just take it."

"Yes," he said. "Let's take it."

When I think of that summer now, I think of it as a kind of long celebration. For me, there was always the possibility of going somewhere. We packed our bags and set off for Maine. I had an assignment in a little town with a snug harbor where just lobster boats and scallop draggers were moored, no luxury yachts. And at the end of the high, stilty wharf there was a lobster pound where we bought lobsters for a reasonable price. We rented a run-down little house-keeping cottage at the edge of a bluff looking out over the water. The tides up there are some of the most dramatic on the continent and, while I went about town doing inter-views, Paul liked to sit in the armless rocker on the little porch and watch the landscape change as the tide rose and fell. "It's like watching a reservoir fill up and empty out, all in just a few hours," he commented one evening after I'd gotten home. The tide was up just then, the dark water tapping against the rock ledges. Small boats and rafts that just hours ago lay aground on the mud flats bobbed in the light breeze. We had a big aluminum pot filled with water on top of the tiny electric stove. We were waiting for the water to boil. The burner was old and it heated the water very slowly, almost imperceptibly. We were in no hurry. We sat and watched the harbor change colors and said little.

We heard the lid on the pot tapping lightly. Paul got up and went in through the sagging screen door. He took the two wriggling green lobsters out of the brown-paper bag, wedged them into the pot and clamped the lid back down. Though it was after eight, the sun was still strong in the sky. When the lobsters had turned red, Paul put them on a big tray and carried it out to the porch, along with a roll of paper towels. He set the tray down on the rickety table between our chairs and went back inside. He had melted a chunk of butter in a small aluminum saucepan, and came back with that and two cold beers. We broke open the shells with our hands, and forced out the meat. The shells piled up on the porch beside us and when it looked as if we had gotten all the meat we could, Paul fished around in the pile and coaxed out the last shreds of the sweet white flesh from the claws and the tail with his fingers and with his tongue.

We sat and finished the beers. The sun had set, but there was still light in the sky. The streetlights down at the wharf had gone on, casting a peaceful reflection into the water. Paul rose and took my hand. "Come on," he said and he led me into the darkened cottage, to the narrow bed with its worn-down mattress, where we made cautious, grateful love.

The summer opened out that way. We went to the

Cape and to Maine again and also to Vermont for a long weekend to camp in our tent beside a wilderness lake. As we both grew stronger, we grew more confident.

If there is a broader lesson in all this for me, it has to do with the nature of truth and how we regard what we believe to be the truth at any particular moment. And how it evolves. At that time, we lost the word *cancer* from our vocabulary. Except when we said it to each other, every once in a while, lying in bed at night or driving in the car: *"No more cancer!"* we would say, in emphatic disbelief. When we talked, it was never about cancer. It was about our everyday lives, as if they had never been interrupted. There was probably some level on which Paul realized and I realized that this was either denial or escapism. And yet, was it? And if it was, did it matter? We had no symptoms and at last there was something to really recover from in the real sense of healing. There was life to be lived.

It was at the end of the summer that we bought the new house. Paul was back working by then. He was building a boathouse up on the lake and he felt strong and looked vigorous. I was getting used to this: Paul getting up in the morning, early, putting on his jeans and flannel shirt and going downstairs to fry up eggs and potatoes in the black skillet, eating them with lots of ketchup. While he ate, he jotted notes in the tiny spiral notebook that he always kept in the breast pocket of his work shirt. When he finished breakfast, he washed his plate in the sink and then sat by the back door to lace up his boots, which made Dune prance in anticipation, which in turn made Paul laugh. Then he'd stand up, put on his hat, which hung by the back door, stick his pencil in under the bow of his glasses and go out to his truck, opening the door to let Dune rush up onto the seat ahead of him. After a couple of weeks of watching him go through this routine, so achingly familiar, I felt as if he'd never been sick. Could this be the same man who lived in that cluttered attic room, the same man who hung his head in public and spoke to no one?

Soon, he was bringing home money. We were working on the checkbook together again. This sounds funny to me now, but it's hard to describe what it felt like then. Watching his hair grow back out, watching his body return to its normal parameters, those things were wonderful, but it was the money that seemed to make the difference. Not in a material sense so much as that it made him feel useful, made him feel he had a purpose in life, that he wasn't just living off of me, which he had not liked very much. And for me it meant maybe we could stop worrying, at least about money. All these things signaled to both of us that we could start once again to think more than a few weeks ahead. After almost a three-year hiatus, we could start to plan a future.

And so we bought the new house. It wasn't that we had been house-hunting. We loved Bide-a-wee and hated the thought of leaving it, but it was small. We were always thinking of ways to add onto it. Even now, on top of Paul's bookcase, there are half a dozen or more rolled-up drawings he did for possible additions to the little house. But every time we started to get serious, something happened. Adding on takes a lot of time, and for a carpenter, that time comes out of time he could spend making money doing the same work for someone else. So we weren't actually looking, but the need was there. And the house, a long Victorian farmhouse, was on the main road down in the village, just a mile from Bide-a-wee. We drove by it every day, with a kind of longing. An old couple, Ralph and Uriel Bemis, had lived there for years, in fact, they'd run it as a chicken farm since the 1920s. First Ralph died and Uriel lived on for a couple of years after that. Then she died. They had no children. We drove by one day and there was a FOR SALE sign on the lawn. We'd never been inside.

"Want to make an appointment, just to see what it looks like?" Paul asked.

"Great idea. It's probably the only chance we'll ever have to see what the rooms are like," I said and called the realtor as soon as I got to my desk the next morning.

We really weren't thinking of buying it, but as one of our friends said, when they walked into it shortly after we bought it, "This is a Paul and Edie house if I ever saw one," and that might have been what we both silently thought as we walked through the rooms, dark and dingy from the long years of marginal upkeep, but, with the broad windows and old doors, full of promise.

It was August when we went to look at it, and outside the windows the full blooms from the tall hydrangea trees pressed against the screens. The kitchen was a big bare room, a metal sink bolted to the wall and no cabinets. Paul stooped and lifted the stained yellow linoleum up from the corner. "Look at this, Bear," he said. Underneath was brand-new fir flooring, never even sanded, just put down and covered with the now-aging linoleum. "All we need to do is sand and urethane it." Such discoveries are like secret treasures. The real estate agent had no clue that there might be value under that ugly floor. We climbed down the creaking old steps into the cellar and had to duck our heads to get inside. Paul began to press his hands against the timbers and poke his knife into their centers. In an old pie safe, I found mason jars full of faded cherries and a bottle of champagne with a motheaten label and a date that *looked* like 1862, the same date the house was supposed to have been built. "Hide that," Paul said and I stuck it in the very back of the safe, behind a lot of faded plastic cemetery flowers—Ralph had taken care of the cemetery next door for years. Paul found a section of the sill in the barn was rotten, but other than that the old building was sound. I followed him back up the uncertain steps and he closed the hatch behind me. "Let's go back upstairs," he said. The real estate agent was politely sitting in her car while we roamed about.

The upstairs was small, only two bedrooms, but there was a lengthy stretch of unfinished area. One part of this expanse was a big room off the second bedroom.

"My God, look at the size of it," I said, walking in. It was almost as big as the whole downstairs at Bide-a-wee.

"This could be our bedroom, H," Paul said.

The floor was rough, like the floor of a barn. There were two big stew pots at different places on the floor, obviously catching leaks. But the light was right. It came in through the dormer window, which was big, with four paned windows that opened outward. Ralph must have put it in. "Maybe they were going to make it into a bed-room at one point," I said. "Why else would you put a dormer into an attic space?"

"I don't know," Paul said, and then after a while: "It would make a great room."

We went from window to window, exploring the views. In the field to the east was a flock of sheep. It was a familiar village sight. The land belonged to this farm but the sheep belonged to our friend David, a farmer who lived nearby. Short on open space at his own farm, he often pastured them here. Whenever we drove by, we enjoyed the sight of these burly black-and-tan ewes working away at the green grass. We knew if we bought this, we could enjoy them at our leisure.

The room had a door at each end and a tiny unpainted south-facing window, the casing stained from condensation. Most of the room was under the roof, so the walls were slanted. Paul leaned lightly against one of the strong-looking, rough-sawn rafters. "We could put a roof window in here. It would let in the morning sun," he said. "And we could see the sheep better."

He cranked open one of the dormer windows. The warm August air moved in. The house had been closed up since Uriel died, and it smelled musty. The west windows looked out over the old cemetery next door. It's a pretty plot, even prettier from that vantage point. A shiny black iron fence with a heart-shaped design surrounded it, and the headstones, mostly from the last century, leaned a little, this way and that. Paul put his arm around me. "Quiet neighbors," he said, his voice lifting up in an urging kind of way.

In order to buy it, we had to take out a mortgage. At Bide-a-wee, we had no mortgage at all, which had made the past couple of years easier for us, financially. But it had not been all that easy. Aside from the fact that Paul had not been able to work (and since he was self-employed, he received no compensation until much later, when he was able to collect disability), there had been the medical bills. Somewhere around this point, sometime before we went to look at the house, we sat down at the kitchen table with our little calculator and a three-inch-thick stack of what the insurance company calls "work sheets"—to us these were simply an acknowledgment of their payment to the doctors, hospitals, medical-supply places. Hardly a day went by that one of these work sheets didn't arrive in our mailbox. At the very beginning of Paul's illness we sat down with each one as it arrived and went over the columns carefully, as if it were our own bill. And, much as with other bills, we found occasional errors. But the work sheets began to come so often, while we were simultaneously dealing with the trauma of the illness, that we eventually simply left them in a heap on the desk, hardly glancing at them. So when we sat down that day—probably during a lull, when things were looking quiet and the healing had set in—we began to reflect on things. Just how much had this illness cost? we suddenly wondered. Some of the bills had been more remarkable than others. A single visit to Dana-Farber, with scans and X rays and a brief, ten-minute visit with Jack, sometimes ran to $600. Just one of Paul's lung operations had been $16,000 for the surgery alone, not including the hospital stay and all the rigmarole that goes along with it (and not including the anesthesia, which we were always mystified to find was not covered by our insurance. How could this be considered a frill? we always wondered. Could you opt *not* to have anesthesia?). In any case, when we sat down to figure this, Paul punching in the numbers as I sorted through the sheets, the total came up an astonishing quarter of a million dollars. It was so astonishing that we went through and totaled it up all over again. Yes, $260,000, a frightening figure. What would have happened to us without health insurance? We had paid only a fraction of that amount, and yet even a small percentage of it represented a financial burden to us.

Thinking back on all the financial pressures we had at the time, we must have agonized over our decision to buy this house, and yet I don't remember that we did. I do remember that on our way to the bank to talk to the loan officer about the possibility of such a mortgage I had said to Paul, "Do you think this is crazy?"

And he said, "Maybe, but I don't think the bank's going to loan us money if they think it's crazy. Let's let them decide."

At the bank, a woman with the perfect poker face of a good banker asked us the pertinent questions as she scribbled things on a form. When she asked Paul about his income he said he hadn't made any money in two years. She looked at him with a straight face, waiting for his explanation. "I've been sick," he said. "But I'm better now. I should be back to normal soon." He knew not to say the word *cancer*.

The bankers had been doubtful, but in the end they lent us the money.

On the night of the closing we sat on the screened porch in folding chairs. It was dusk. The hydrangeas were hanging heavy with creamy blossoms as huge and dense as fruit, in such full bloom that their flowers were about all we could see as we looked out. "Oh, I know!" Paul jumped up from his chair and disappeared. I heard him going down into the cellar. He came back with that ancient bottle of champagne we had hidden in the pie safe. "We need to celebrate," he said. The light-green bottle was thick with the dust of its more than a century in the cellar. He took the blue bandanna out of his back pocket and rubbed the bottle, then flipped on the overhead light and let it shine through the glass. The wine looked awful, as if there was algae growing inside. We made faces at each other and then laughed. "Oh, God," he said and set the bottle back down on the floor. He thought for a moment before he said, "How about a beer?"

It was insane, perhaps, buying that house. Thinking about it now, I can hardly believe nothing truly catastrophic happened as a result. But Paul needed these projects, he needed a house to create. While he was on chemotherapy, fixing up the barn had kept him going. We said to many friends who greeted our news with surprise, "Well, we'll just have to keep buying buildings to fix up. It's the only way Paul knows how to heal."

As soon as we bought the house we started tearing it

apart, beginning with the kitchen ceiling. Because of Paul's lungs, I did most of the tearing out, wearing a mask to protect me from the plaster dust and remembering the lessons I learned when we tore the walls out of Bide-a-wee.

While I worked on the ceiling, Paul started to craft the cabinets, working over at the barn. We had a stash of tiger-stripe oak boards we had bought at auction—we knew they'd come in handy for something and this was it. Sometimes, when I was in my office at the barn, I would stop and watch him work. I felt as if I was seeing a mirage or living in a dream. His muscles were back and his arms and neck were brown again. To make his work easier, he had moved one of his table saws into the gutted kitchen and begun the frame for the cabinets. At night I swept off the saw bed, cranked the blade down and used it like a countertop, cooking carrots and potatoes and onions and chicken all in one pot over a one-burner hot plate. We sat on the sawhorses while we ate and talked about where the cabinets would go and how to finish off the counters. It reminded us of tearing out Bide-a-wee and of the many new beginnings which that had brought us.

We enjoyed that summer fully and completely, and I'll never be sorry for it. I say this because there were a couple of junctures in Paul's illness where we really wondered whether we had been treated thoughtfully by the doctors, although this only came into focus in retrospect. After Paul's second lung operation in April, the doctors apparently finally came up with a new diagnosis. The pathology report on the tumors removed from the lungs came back as metastatic malignant melanoma, one of the most deadly forms of cancer. It was in a sense what we'd been waiting for: the final diagnosis. But we weren't told about that then. Instead, we had Jack's tentative agreement that Paul was in remission.

When we finally did hear the news, it was late fall. It was one of those things that was slid at us, an oblique hit, driven in by Dr. Knoop when he discovered the tumors in the lungs had returned. "Of course, with melanoma, you can expect this," he said, or something like that, a sentence that implied that we knew this new diagnosis.

"Melanoma?" Paul and I said it just about together and looked at each other, stunned.

"Yes," Dr. Knoop said, "surely you were told?" We said no, again together.

And he looked surprised, but not overly so. There were so many doctors involved in that last part, it was hard to know who was in charge. Jack had faded into the background, although he was still the oncologist in charge of Paul's case.

Whether it was carelessness, an oversight, that we were never told, or whether it was a judgment call on Jack's part, we'll never know, but I feel sure that if we had been told in April, we never would have lived through the fullness of the summer and grown strong enough to buy our new house, which is what we did and which is where I now live, accepting it almost daily as a gift from Paul.

It was some time soon after we bought the house that we learned about the new tumors in the lungs. It was on the same visit with Dr. Knoop that brought us the news about the new diagnosis. One night, as we lay in bed, I found a tumor on Paul's back. It was long and cylindrical, like a pencil stub beneath the skin. The next day we raced in to see Jack, who calmly told us it was nothing to worry about and sent us home.

"I would have at least expected he would have removed the damn thing," Paul said on the way home, disgusted.

Not long after that, Paul took my hand and pressed it into his stomach, forcefully enough so I could feel the tumor he could feel, a hard knot, big around as a quarter. "Does it hurt?" I asked him.

"No," he said, "it doesn't hurt."

We said nothing else about it. What was there to say? What amount of talk could change these things? It wasn't as if it were a problem that could be solved, that if we talked long enough we would come up with the answer. We just wanted to hang on to the life we were trying to build. When Paul talked about his illness at all, what he said was quite simple: "I just need to keep working. And praying."

Finally Jack approached us with the news that Paul would be eligible to enroll in an experimental treatment program called interleukin-2. I never fully understood how it worked but it sounded to me as if they would take Paul's blood out, spin it in a machine to cleanse it and put it back in. Something like that.

The program was done in groups. Jack was able to squeeze Paul into the group scheduled to start in January. In preparation, they needed a complete set of scans, scheduled early the morning after Christmas. To be sure we would be there on time, we went down the evening before and spent Christmas night with my cousin in Wellesley.

Her guest bedroom had become a kind of home for us. Another family was there that night for dinner. Their children plus my cousin's made six or seven, all of them sharing Christmas presents with one another. We said our hellos and carried our suitcase upstairs to our room and closed the door. Paul was tired. He took off his clothes, leaving on his long underwear, and burrowed under the familiar green quilt. It seemed he was asleep immediately. I sat up in bed and read the Sunday papers. I wasn't tired. I could feel the warmth from the furnace pump up through the grate in the floor and smell the good dinner smells coming up too. I had spent so many nights in this room. The night before my operation I slept there, and said good-bye to any hope of ever having children. And all during Paul's stay in intensive care, during his lung operations, I slept there, my fear for him moving into the room with me like an actual presence. I had said such fervent prayers there that the room seemed, in spite of its odd, hodgepodge furniture, almost a sacred place. I finally felt drowsy, so I snapped off the light and slid down next to Paul, his body hot with night fevers. I took his hand and drifted off to sleep, listening to the happy sounds of the children downstairs being surprised and delighted once again by the rituals of Christmas.

Instead of the predicted snow and sleet, the next morning was mild, like a spring morning, and we went out for a walk at six, when the streets there are still quiet. The shops were still decorated for Christmas and the long strings of white bulbs twinkled overhead in the bare branches of the tall maples that grow near the sidewalks. Our walk was cut short by Paul's cough, which was getting worse each day.

By nine o'clock we had found our way to Dr. Eberlein's office. It was empty, so we sat in the burgundy chairs and waited until a nurse came out. Paul introduced himself. A quick flash of recognition came into her face when he said his name. She handed him the consent form. "Read it over carefully. I'll be back in a little while. All three of us will have to sign it."

It was four pages long, in small type. The fourth page began: ". . . This new therapy is not proven to be effective in the treatment of your disease. . . . It is not possible to say whether or not you will benefit from the use of this therapy." And so on. The course of the treatment and a long explanation of the various (and multiple) side effects, ranging from lightheadedness and tingling in the fingertips to collapsed lung and heart attack, were outlined. Death was listed as a "rare and unexpected side effect."

"Side effect?" Paul said, underscoring the words with his finger. "That's kind of a major effect, isn't it?"

I laughed, shaking my head. We had our chairs pushed together and were reading this long document slowly and carefully.

"Remember Mike Sheehan?" Paul said, when he'd gotten to the end of the last page.

"Yes, of course," I said. I remembered how Mike and

Carla Sheehan had haunted me then. Mike seemed so nonchalant about the whole thing. Five rounds of chemo, thirty-six rounds of radiation, umpteen surgeries. He had a little shrug-it-off laugh while he told it all. It was a revelation to us then, that there could be such a road lying ahead of us. Now we had lived it. I remember the way he sort of tossed that consent form across the bed at me and how I kept thinking, my God, this man is going to *die,* how can he act this way? Now I understood, I understood completely. There is a robe that you wear, a way of accepting all this as the context of your life. It wasn't as if there were choices.

"I feel the way he did," Paul said. "I'm the guinea pig now. But maybe if I go through with this, I can help whoever comes after me."

When the woman came back, we all signed at the bottom of the fourth page.

She asked if we had any questions. Surely there was a lot about this that we didn't know, that we couldn't anticipate. But we both sat there dumbly, just looking at her. We knew how little the answers had helped us in the past. Finally, Paul said, "I guess not."

Hours later, we moved, trancelike, back upstairs to the waiting room at the clinic. The receptionist told us to have a seat, that Jack would be coming soon. A small man with a gray mustache and a beret was standing next to her desk. I could feel his intensity as soon as we walked into the room. We had interrupted him. He rested his fist on the desktop. "Look," he was saying, "my wife needs to have this X ray *now*. This is an *emergency*." I could almost feel his anger creep in under my skin as he talked; I had felt that way so many times.

"Please have a seat," the receptionist said, not really looking at him. "Everyone here is sick. She'll just have to wait her turn."

It had taken me so long to realize that the incredible sense of urgency inside my heart, the feeling of extreme danger, had no place here, inside these walls, where everyone felt the same rage and anguish. The need to *do* something, to turn the tide, belonged to everyone here. We all just had to wait in line.

Jack came out. "Hey, buddy, how's it going? Long day?" he said to Paul, resting his hand on Paul's knee.

Paul nodded.

Jack asked if we had gone over and signed the consent form and then he said, "We should have the results of the scans tomorrow. I'll give you a call if need be. Otherwise, see ya Tuesday."

We got back home around nine o'clock. The house was still torn apart, though things were nearing the finish line. Paul and his helper, Bryan, had started to install the oak cabinets, bringing them over from the barn in the back of the truck, one by one. The half-made counters were heaped with drills and screwdrivers and electrical cords, and the floors were littered with more tools and scrap. We picked our way across the room and Paul headed straight for bed. I put the kettle on the hot plate to make some herb tea, turned out the light and went into the living room to sit in my rocker, waiting for the water to boil. I left the lights off. I had opened the curtains, which we usually kept closed because we are so close to the road. We have a streetlight not far from the living-room window, and its glow, combined with the moonlight, shone in and gave the purple flowers on the table a strange brilliance. Outside, in the dimness, I could see the sheep standing by the fence, the sounds of their bells small and distant. Pretty soon I could hear the water boiling, so I made my way through the dark into the kitchen. I found a cup on the counter and went back to the chair with my tea and sat there, warming my hands around the steaming cup. I guess I was there for a long time. Dune slept beside the chair, on her side, her legs stuck out in front of her, her breathing soft and rhythmic. The furnace rumbled on and off, on and off. After the clock struck twelve, I stopped counting. "Honey?" Paul called from upstairs, his voice so soft I thought it was my imagination. I went up and sat on the edge of the bed next to him. The windows in that room let in only a little light, enough for shadows. "I'm scared," I said, and the tears I'd been holding back let go. He sat up and held me and he said, "I am too."

I don't know where I got the notion, but I had a small dread that if Paul's cancer had gone too far he would not be eligible for the interleukin program. In fact, though the scans confirmed the tumors in the lungs and the tumor in his stomach, which had grown two inches in less than a month, the head scan bore the gravest news: brain tumors, five of them. I heard Jack saying all this to me on the phone when he called me the next morning. His voice was like a monotone, telling me that they couldn't take Paul in the interleukin program, that they would try some other kind of chemo, that Paul shouldn't drive or operate any machinery because he might have seizures. I thought of it all—the round hardness in his stomach, the lumps in his lungs pushing against his bronchial tubes, making him choke, the lump on his back, and now the five mysterious intruders in his brain. I felt a kind of dizziness, a circling confusion, as if there were three or four voices talking at me into the one phone. Jack was telling me about possible treatments—radiation, chemo—but it wasn't making any sense. Hot tears washed down my face as he talked. I knew where Paul was. He was in our new kitchen, measuring for the last cabinet. He was trying to finish before he started the treatments on Tuesday. I wanted him to be hearing all this with me, so that I could see his face calmly listening to the news, taking it in and accepting it. I wanted to know that he could understand it, because I could not.

9

I never imagined that dying could be so hard. There are so many other ways to die. I kept thinking about that. We rented Bide-a-wee to a young woman whose husband was killed by a hunter. She had told me the story in bits and pieces, her eyes still blank from shock. She had been with him. They were out together in their truck. This happened in Maine and both of them were barely thirty years old. They had stopped by the side of the road to pick up some wood they had cut. It was dusk. The two of them got out and began to pick up a log, one on each end. *Bam.* The hunter had mistaken Jim for a deer, or so he said later. The hunter was also drunk. But what did it matter? *Bam.* Shot and killed, just like that.

I kept thinking about the passengers in that jet that had just taken off from Hawaii, bound for Sydney. I read the description in the papers, how they had taken off, were making the final ascent, a beautiful blue-sky day, the plane rising up above the puffy clouds. The flight attendants were in the aisle, passing out drinks. All of a sudden, *bam,* a hole ripped out of the side of the plane. Nine people, sucked into the air. The reporters quoted passengers describing what it was like to look over at the seats beside them and to see the people gone, to see nothing but sky racing past. No trace of them was found except a running shoe that washed up on shore.

I kept thinking about an accident I had come upon late one Friday afternoon, driving a winding back road in the Berkshires. The rescue people were just removing the man from the twisted wreck. He was dead. In the backseat I could see his red suitcase and a couple of tennis rackets. He was on his way somewhere for a weekend. He didn't know he was going to die that day. Neither did the others. They had things on their minds, about a woodpile, about an adventure to Australia, about a weekend trip. They were all young and they were not thinking about dying. Is it better to die that way?

By that time we had been thinking about dying for a long time. We were reading books about dying and we got very irritated with the ones that seemed to give the message that dying was the booby prize, as if life were some kind of competition and if you have all the right answers, you wouldn't die, you couldn't die. Books that said that if you're dying of cancer or some other incurable disease, it's somehow your fault, that you didn't *try* hard enough or make the right choices—you didn't eat the right things or you didn't live your life right or something was unsettled in your heart.

We could only speak for ourselves. When you have cancer, you do wonder how it happened, you think about it a lot. We are used to knowing the reasons for things. Paul was not a drinker nor a smoker. He was strong and completely fit. He lived near a nuclear power plant for ten years, that was the only possible answer. We asked Jack once, and he said, "We can't speculate on the cause. No one really knows. We're too busy trying to fix it." I asked him about the nuclear plant, and he said, "Oh, that's impossible to prove."

It wasn't that we wanted proof, as if for a lawsuit. It was that we wanted to end the mystery, the mystery that kept getting darker and more overwhelming.

I knew by this time that we were coming to the end. I called Jack. He still had never told us that Paul would die. He had never told us how much time Paul had left.

"Jack," I said, "I need to know what we are facing."

"Well," he said, "it is hard to say." His voice was subdued. Paul and I often remarked on how, whenever there was bad news, Jack wasn't there. He had proved himself to be relentlessly upbeat, a master of euphemisms. He had never talked with us about death. Paul thought that this was the Harvard in him, that it represented, for Jack, a kind of failure he couldn't endure, but I found it hard to believe that a man with an ego like that would choose to be in this dark branch of medicine. The telephone line was

silent for a bit before Jack went on, "Every patient is different and Paul has certainly surprised us many times. But he
hasn't responded to any of the treatments and with that
amount of cancer in him, it is unlikely he will live very
long."

"But Jack"—I felt like screaming into the phone—
"what do you mean by 'very long'?" He had never yet
used the word *die,* and in fact he never did.

"One, two, maybe three months? It really is very hard
to tell."

"Is it the brain tumors that are the most dangerous?" I
worried most about them. It was very hard for me, every
day, to leave Paul alone in the house. I worried that he
would fall or have a seizure while I wasn't there.

"No, I don't really worry about them, though of
course anything can happen when something is growing in
your brain. I still feel it is the lung tumors that will, um, do
him in. They are growing rapidly."

I didn't answer, so he went on, after a long pause. "I
think he has maybe a month left of being well, well enough
to do things and go places and enjoy things. You and Paul
have talked about going away. If you want to do that, you
should go, go tomorrow, don't waste a day. Every day that
passes, he'll be sicker."

My sister, Chris, lives in the mountains in Washington state. I asked him if that would be too far to go.

"No," he said, "do it."

Before I hung up, he said, "Edie? Edie, there's something I have to tell you. I hate to tell you on the phone."

What could he tell me that would be worse than what he already had told me?

"What is it?" I asked, feeling an absurd sense of dread.

"It's honestly very hard for me to tell you this, but I am going to be leaving Dana Farber."

"Oh, my God," I said, seriously surprised. "When? Where are you going?"

"I'm going to a small hospital in Michigan. I won't be leaving until May but I'll be changing my patients over before then. I would recommend that you find a doctor closer to your home. The facilities here are great, but there really isn't that much more we can offer you that your local doctor can't give you just as well."

There was a pause. "I feel a little like I'm jumping ship," he said.

After three years, we had learned how to talk to each other. There was a closeness that is inevitable in spite of a doctor's need to stay apart. You can't, he couldn't. In so much time spent together, there's a lot of silence to fill. We knew about Jack's wife and his new baby and we knew about all the different cars he considered before he finally settled on the Saab. We knew about his grandmother's cooking and where he had grown up and what his brother was like. We knew a lot. He, of course, knew a great deal more about both of us. And beyond all that, I could tell how much Jack liked Paul, in spite of his efforts to remain aloof. I was surprised when I heard him say this, even though it was close to what Paul and I had felt. And his telling me about the move made me feel compassion for his situation. "No," I said, trying to hide my concern. "I know Paul won't think you're deserting him."

"Do me a favor," I said.

"What's that?"

"Paul is home right now. Would you call him and tell him yourself?" I knew Jack wanted me to do it; he always wanted me to tell Paul the bad news.

"Okay, I'll do that," he said.

He never did. I called Paul a short while later and talked about taking a trip. "Jack thinks it would be okay," I said.

"Are you sure?" Paul asked. It was as if we were talking in code. He knew what this meant. The rhythm of our lives for the past three years had been a procession of treatments and surgeries, each one precipitating the next. Except for our summer, there had been no respite.

"Yup, I'm sure. I was thinking about those tickets Chris has for us, remember she said she had a couple of frequent-flyer tickets we could use?"

"You mean go out there, to the mountains?"

"That's what I was thinking. How about it?"

"*Great,*" he said, his voice lifting.

I hesitated, wondering if this was such a good idea. I thought of his daily efforts to feed the sheep and how it tired him. "It might be kind of tiring," I said. "Do you think you'd feel well enough?"

"This is my chance to see those mountains. You know I've always wanted to go out west."

"Yeah, and we *finally* get to fly on a plane together!"

It wasn't that hard to make this into an adventure. Paul was always a willing ally in escape.

By the end of the day I had the name of Dr. Liepman, a doctor from Worcester who kept an office in Peterborough. Several of our friends recommended her and she sounded good. And I had reservations for both of us on a flight out of Boston to Seattle for the next day. Chris was sending the tickets to us Federal Express. And she would be there at the airport to pick us up. She was thrilled. She hadn't seen Paul in over a year. I warned her, but I knew there was no way to prepare her.

The trip to Washington isn't one I want to write about. Paul had never been on an airplane and we had always looked forward to flying somewhere together. He had never been out west, a place he said he dreamed of going. He had never seen mountains, real mountains. These were all things we had planned to do, one day. It was like that now-long-ago train ride to New York City that he and I had taken together. Unfortunately, even though this trip west was far more dramatic than that brief train ride, it lacked the magic. In fact, the entire trip, which lasted only five days, was fraught with horrors.

Paul's face was almost grotesquely bloated and distorted from the medication he was taking. He looked as if he had been beaten up, and it pained me to see him. I'm sure he sensed this, and at the airport he kept his face down as we walked. He refused to use a wheelchair until he slumped down in a waiting area, unable to go any further. I flagged one of the golf carts reserved for elderly passengers and had to explain he was sick, since we were young-looking. On the plane, he went white: I think it was fear, but I'll never know. I just know he couldn't breathe.

It was true that he had trouble breathing all the time, but up in the mountains the condition was aggravated, though oddly none of us could believe it was the altitude. We thought he was dying every time he gasped for breath. He looked sad and scared. Though it was wonderful to be with my sister and her family, and their kindnesses to us were abundant, I couldn't wait to get back. At night I lay awake listening to his labored breathing, afraid he would die there, so very far from home. I longed for those solid, normal, routine moments of our lives, so soothing, so precious to us now. I wanted nothing more than to go home.

There is only one day I recall with pleasure, a cold, crystal-clear day. My sister's husband, Charlie, wanted to take Paul up into the mountains on the snowmobile. So we went, the four of us, on two snowmobiles. Their house is in the Cascade mountains. It is a beautiful area and there are trails all around, up and through the passes. At every turn, there are breathtaking vistas of snow-covered peaks. We climbed and stopped and got off to take pictures and climbed some more. At one point Charlie brought his machine to rest up against a mound of snow and Chris pulled in behind him. They turned off the engines and the silence seemed even more profound because of it. The snow was deep and the sun was making the edges of the drifts blue-green. Through a gap, we could see numberless sharp ragged peaks fading off into the distance. Paul stood beside me. His breathing was forced, though he had not walked anywhere. He had simply stood up from his seat on the snowmobile. He was wearing a black snowmobile suit, borrowed from Charlie. It hung loosely on him and the hood was cinched tight around his swollen face. But his cheeks were pink from the ride and his eyes were sparkly. We stood looking into the distance. He put his arm around me, weakly. "Oh, H," he said, his voice whispery soft, halting between words for more air, "this is unbelievable. This is the most beautiful place I've ever been."

When we came home, emergencies became more and more frequent. Twice his lungs filled with fluid and he almost drowned. Drowned. That is the word the doctors used. I never really got numb to moments of extreme danger, but I was close. In between, though, he worked on the kitchen. He was not supposed to, of course. Jack had told him not to drive anymore and not to operate any machinery. Paul said he understood about the driving, because if he had a seizure he could hurt someone else. But the tools, he never paid any attention to that. "What am I risking anyway?" was his explanation of why he went on using the tools. He figured his life was already in such jeopardy that being concerned about hurting himself would be silly. And in the meantime he could work, always his salvation.

There's a line in my kitchen floor, a line made by Paul's saw as he cut away the floorboards so he could set in a tile hearth for the wood stove. I sit in my chair beside the stove now and sometimes my eye rests on that line and tears come up. It still hurts to remember him, down on his knees, guiding that circular saw with all his strength, which by then was so diminished that his arms shook as he held on to the metal housing of the screaming, spinning blade. The reason it hurts so to see that line is because it is crooked. Paul's lines were never crooked. But in this case, he was so weak the fact that he cut it at all was the miracle. Whether or not it was straight made no difference. I walked in and saw him trying to cut those hard old floorboards. "Paul!" I said. "For Christ's sake, Paul, stop!"

He let his finger off the trigger and the blade whirled to a stop. He said calmly, though I could feel anger, "This has to be done before the sanders come tomorrow. They're coming whether this gets done or not."

"Well then, let me do it," I said. He knew I knew my way around that saw. He didn't answer. He just started up the saw again and pushed it slowly to where the floor met the wall.

In March, he finished the kitchen. To me, of course, it was the most beautiful kitchen I'd ever seen and I still feel that way. The floors came up pumpkin colored and the glass-fronted cabinets were trimmed in that good oak that he'd planed to a velvet softness. The countertops are sky blue, edged in the same oak, the tiger stripes showing strong. Everything in that room speaks of Paul to me. It humbles me to think of how many options he had at the end of his life. Certainly finishing a kitchen he would likely never use would not have been at the top of every dying man's list. I came home from work one day to find him standing on a stepladder, putting up curtain rods in the living room. "Oh, Paul," I said, distressed to see him up on a step. Ladders and step stools were out. "Get down from there. I can do that."

He came off the ladder and put the drill on the table. "It's okay, Bear," he said, "I want to finish this for you. You know I don't like to leave anything unfinished."

I always dreaded coming home from work. I never quite knew what I would find. I called Paul two or three times during the day and always went home for lunch when I wasn't out on the road. But still, every night as I pulled in the driveway and headed into the kitchen, I felt a kind of restrained panic. One day in early April I came home to find Paul wasn't downstairs the way he usually was. I called and he answered from upstairs, "I'm up here, come up please."

I went upstairs. Paul was in the guest bedroom, under the green-and-blue afghan his Aunt Elsie had knit for us for our wedding.

"Help me," he said. He looked really scared.

"Are you in pain?" I asked him as I grabbed the phone and dialed the first of three numbers I had for Dr. Liepman.

"No," he said, "nothing hurts but something's wrong. I keep throwing up, no warning."

We had only seen Dr. Liepman once, a kind of get-acquainted visit. I felt as if I was calling a stranger and longed to hear Jack's voice on the other end of the line. Dr. Liepman directed me to the hospital in Worcester, a confusing combination of highways and back roads and then, once we got to the city, a variety of lefts and rights. I wrote it all on the back of an envelope. "It will take you about an hour," she said. "I'll be there to meet you."

I cranked the passenger seat back for Paul and he lay blessedly asleep all the way as I drove in near panic, searching each dark intersection for the blue hospital signs. As we crossed through the automatic doors of the emergency room at the Worcester hospital I felt a further sense of panic, that somehow we had made the wrong decision. No one here knew Paul. At Dana-Farber, they had three thick notebooks filled with his records, his name on the spine of each book. The nurses knew him there. Many of the doctors did too. He was a very familiar face. And Dana-Farber was such a state-of-the-art facility. This place looked like nothing of the sort. Oh, God, I prayed as we made our way to the desk, please be kind to us.

There were tests and long waits there in the emergency room. At last, they showed us the X rays. It was the tumor in his stomach. Why hadn't I thought of that? Jack had made so light of it, as if it were not worth thinking about. Paul had taken my hand a night or two before and placed it on his stomach. I'd spread my fingers wide, searching for the perimeters and even as wide as I could stretch, I couldn't fit my hand around this growth. Now the X rays showed it, a glowing white dome, blocking his bowels. They also found that he had pneumonia. I knew that patients with lung tumors like Paul's almost never survive pneumonia. They took him upstairs and put him in a room by himself. I drove home alone in the middle of the night.

Dr. Liepman turned out to be a blessing for Paul. Compassionate and attentive, she came to see him twice a day, Saturdays and Sundays too, the two weeks he was in that hospital. After he came home, even though there was no crisis, she came to visit him, making the long drive from Worcester to Chesham as if it were all part of her job. When she told him that he had very little time left, he told me she had tears in her eyes and I think that meant a lot to him.

Because of the blockage, he would live out the rest of his life on clear liquids, and "You can't live very long on clear liquids," she told me gently the evening of his third night in the hospital. We sat in a narrow lounge, facing an aquarium where brightly colored fish darted back and forth in yellowish water. She was thin and young and I'd heard from the nurses that she had small children and kept horses on a farm outside the city. It made me wonder how she had time to be so attentive. She was sincere when she said to me, "Paul is a special kind of person, I can tell. Cancer is the cruelest disease and it should never, never happen to a man like Paul."

She suggested I tell his family to come down to the hospital, which I did. They all came, his mother and father standing tentatively beside the bed as if they were at a social occasion where they weren't sure how to act. His brother, Donald, came as well. He had not yet acknowledged Paul's sickness, either through card or visit. He is tall, his body hard and brown from his work on his dairy farm. He actually looked contrite as he entered the room and said, "Hello, Paul," and then sat in the blue plastic-covered armchair beside the bed, his big veined hands folded in his lap, his head turned, staring out the window at the ascending rows of triple-decker houses and the vinyl-sided church next to the hospital, where the message was spelled out in giant black capital letters: JESUS LOVES YOU.

My parents came also. They were elderly by then, and frail, but they drove up from New Jersey and found their way to the hospital through the confusing streets of Worcester. The unfolding of Paul's illness, week after week, month after month, year after year, had undone them. They did what they could to help, sometimes coming to stay at the house and care for the dogs while Paul and I were in Boston or frequently sending flowers or funny cards. They telephoned almost daily—my father often called Paul and they had private chats. Overall, they were devastated by what we were facing. We all went in to see Paul separately for brief visits and then congregated in the canteen downstairs, where we groped for conversation, sidestepping the gravity of why we had all come together.

But Paul did get better. Dr. Liepman and the other doctors couldn't explain it to us nor to themselves, but the blockage cleared itself and the pneumonia improved so that he could come home. He did know, though, that he was coming home to die. He was as graceful about this as he had been about everything else in his life, showing not anger or bitterness but only disappointment.

While he had been in the hospital, my cousins had begun work to finish the big bedroom that Paul had started the previous fall. After we bought the house, Paul put in a big roof window that looked up at the overhanging limbs of the big pine out front and at the height of the sky. He insulated the space and put up sheetrock, but then, after the brain tumors were discovered at Christmas, we closed the door on it. I hoped he had forgotten the unfinished project. It was enough he was trying to finish the kitchen. But my Aunt Peg resurrected it. "What would it take to get that room finished?" she asked me one evening over the phone. My aunt could see the need for us to have a spare bedroom where she or my parents could come and stay, or perhaps a nurse, if it came to that. "It could mean the difference between Paul staying home and his having to be in a hospital or a nursing home," she said.

I could see she was right. "It would take a lot," I said.

There was spackling and trim, floors and carpet, paint and paper. There are a lot of cousins, though, and they divvied up the jobs so that by the time we arrived home, there was a frenzy of work going on in the house, sanding and sawing and hammering, all of which made Paul uncomfortable, perhaps miserable. He hated to think of other people doing his work and I almost called it off.

After he came home, he was on oxygen a lot of the time. The air came from one of those big weigh-a-ton machines that seems to breathe too, in great whooshing, sighing gasps. It had lengths of tubing, with nasal prongs that hung over his ears, so that he could move around the house fairly easily. He tried not to use it unless he had to and I think he could have made himself more comfortable if he'd given in to that need, but he hated the tubing, which tugged on him like a leash or a tether.

He seemed, in an odd way, to be getting better. His

appetite was good and he had put on some of the weight he'd lost at the hospital. The pneumonia was gone and though his breathing was quite musical (one visitor rushed to the window to look up to the sky for the geese he thought he'd just heard—it was Paul breathing; another asked, Where is the cat I keep hearing?) he was able to walk out to the mailbox every day and get the mail, which was what he looked forward to. Occasionally he brought in a few sticks of wood for the woodstove, although he paid for it in the spells of breathlessness that followed. Most important, though, David had left the sheep in the pasture that winter, for it was an open winter. Paul took great pride in going out in the mornings and wheeling bales of hay and cans of dried corn out to them in the field. Animals took to Paul. They sensed his gentleness, and whenever he came out the door, these sheep baaed and rushed to the fence, bells clanging against their chests.

It took about a month to get that room finished. Cousin George and his wife, Hazel, came and spent a beautiful sunny Sunday hanging the wallpaper, a pattern of tiny blue roses climbing a cream-colored background. Paul had selected it. After he got out of the hospital, we went together to the paint store and thumbed through the books, marking about a dozen that we liked, and then narrowing it down to two. Paul decided on this one—he loved the roses and he also thought it would be an easy pattern to hang. It was one of our very last outings.

I was up at four in the morning for several days, painting the walls and woodwork. A muscle-bound young man finally came and laid the carpet, a dove gray. When the room was done, it was glorious, with light and air coming in from all sides. The dormer to the west looked out on the old stone monuments in the cemetery next door. A small south window let in sun nearly all day, and to the east there was the new roof window that cranked open so that, though we could not see the sheep in our field as we'd imagined—we could only see sky—we could hear, day and night, the ringing of the bells they wore around their necks, a heavenly sound.

Ned, a smiling, brown-skinned hospice volunteer, came the next evening. Paul sat downstairs in the living room, hitched to the oxygen machine, while Ned and I hefted the bed and two dressers into the new room. He helped me connect a fresh package of tubing to Paul's oxygen line so that it would reach further down the hall. After he left, Paul made his way up the stairs, one step at a time. He stood in the doorway. I was a little apprehensive. He had not liked knowing that other people had done the work that rightly was his. He smiled. "Looks good, Honey Bear," he said.

We slept there that night. In the morning I woke early. The room was so much brighter than the north-facing room where we'd been sleeping. Sunlight fell through the roof window onto the carpet. "Listen," he said. We could hear phoebes and robins and nuthatches making a racket outside the windows, a dimension of the morning we had greatly missed since moving from Bide-a-wee, where the sounds of the woods had been so much closer to us. With an effort, Paul sat up on the edge of the bed and then rose to his feet. He looked out the window above the bed. The window was even with the top of the cherry tree. The deep pink blossoms filled the glass. "Oh, Bear," he said, his voice even softer than usual. "This is nice."

Two weeks later, his breathing grew worse. He struggled desperately to catch his breath, the way he had while we were in the mountains. He sat on the edge of the bed, leaning over to draw in more air.

"Don't you think I should call Dr. Liepman?" I was almost shaking with fear. *Please, let me call,* I was praying.

"*No,*" he said, his voice emphatic. "I'm okay. This is just a spell. You know it's just a spell."

It was hard to know. How many times, late at night, had we rushed to the emergency room as he gasped, only to be sent home by the doctor on call? All of them gave us a variation on the same theme: "You just don't have a lot of room left in those lungs."

I did phone the doctor the next morning, as soon as I got to work. I told her about his night. I heard her start to say, "He's dying," but I cut her off before she could get the whole word out. After all that time, I still couldn't believe that it was happening, maybe because there *had* been all that time. She repeated it though: "Edie, he is dying, he is suffocating. His body is young and healthy and it is fighting against him. We've got to make him stop fighting.

"Think carefully, Edie," she went on. "Does Paul want to die at home—do you want him to die at home?"

I didn't think, I simply said, "Of course."

She said she would arrange for a morphine pump that would deliver a constant dose of the drug and gradually relax him. "It will make his breathing easier and then, eventually, it will just stop." There was a silence on the line. Her words took my breath away. She broke the tension by saying, "Go home, be with him now, forget the work. You need to be with him now."

"How long are you talking about?" I asked, fighting to keep a reasonable tone in my voice.

"We're talking a few days. Go home and tell Paul what I have told you," she said.

I was working that day at the magazine offices. It was early, everyone was coming in, getting coffee, getting settled into the day. I closed the door to my office and began to sob. A friend came in and held me and I tried to tell her what Dr. Liepman had said but it came out nonsense syllables. More friends came in and gathered near me. Someone massaged my shoulders. Someone held my hand. No matter how many there were, there could never have been enough.

I went home and went upstairs. Paul was sitting up in bed, his one pillow scrunched up behind him. Sunlight streamed in through the dormer windows and lit up his head from behind. I sat down on the bed next to him and held his hand, no longer able to stop the tears that fell on my shirt in a stream. He looked back at me, his eyes dark and intent. I couldn't imagine telling him what Dr. Liepman had told me.

It was Friday, the start of the three-day Memorial Day

weekend. I was scared. I called Cousin George. I was confused. I had known Paul was dying for years, really. When Dr. Liepman said, "He is dying"—did she mean *now*?

George came that night, bringing pizza. Though Paul was on the oxygen all the time then, he still got dressed every day and he always came downstairs. Friday had been no exception, even though he now had the additional encumbrance of the morphine pump and its tubing to tangle with the oxygen tubes. Still, Paul was buoyed, as always, by George's arrival.

George helped me put the oxygen machine on a dolly so Paul could have greater range and together we pushed it out to the screened porch. We made salad and ate on paper plates, lighting candles when it got dark. When Paul grew tired, we all three went upstairs to the new room and George and I sat on the end of the bed after Paul had settled in under the covers. George took the hymnal from the bookshelf. He wanted to sing, so the two of us sang to Paul—"Faith of our Fathers," "O God, Our Help In Ages Past," "Blessed Assurance." We grew bolder, our voices stronger, with each new selection and Paul lay back on the pillows, smiling and making suggestions when we'd finished. The roof window was cranked open wide to the warm May evening and I somehow felt that the sheep were listening to this, enjoying our cousinly harmony. George said a prayer, a long thanksgiving for Paul, and went to bed. I got in under the covers and slid next to Paul. He touched my hand lightly and we went off to sleep, the sheep bells *ding-dinging* on the night air.

·   ·   ·

The weather turned gorgeous on Sunday—a quintessential summer day with blue skies and puffy white clouds and breezes that pushed the curtains out from the windowsill above Paul's head. He didn't get up that day, except to go to the bathroom. He seemed a little dopey from the morphine. He lay in bed most of the day and I sat in the room with him, where the sun seemed brighter even than outdoors, and the breezes calmer. He dozed on and off. I had been bringing his meals up on a tray and he ate well—hot cereal in the morning, soup and crackers for lunch, chicken and baked potato at dinner, and ice cream, lots and lots of ice cream.

It was undeniably Memorial Day weekend. Friday we had watched out the dormer window as the man who takes care of our town cemeteries mowed the grass around the stones. As he worked, his wife and his two children raked the grass clippings and the pine needles into small piles against the fence.

"Looks like they're getting ready for a parade," Paul said dreamily.

"Yeah," I said, "and we've got ringside seats!"

There was a parade, of sorts, though not the kind we were thinking of. From the window, we watched, all weekend long, people, singly and in pairs, come into the cemetery bringing flowers to the graves of their loved ones.

His breathing seemed much better and I started to relax. There were no visitors, and it was a very peaceful, beautiful day. We sat together in the sunny room—he propped on pillows, dozing on and off, and I next to him in the rocker, reading, holding his hand.

Toward the end of the day, Paul said he couldn't stand the smell of himself anymore and asked if he could take a shower. It had indeed been at least a week, maybe more, since he had bathed. Baths and showers had become hard for him, making him winded from the effort of soaping himself and getting in and out of the tub.

I needed one too, so I said, "Come on, take one with me and I'll do all the work."

It was hard for him, with all the tubing, but he got out of his pajamas and stepped carefully into the tub, where the spray of warm water met him. I stepped in after him and lathered his soft, smooth skin. We had not made love in some months (except for one very tender time after he got out of the hospital in Worcester) and I was surprised to realize that I had not seen his body naked for quite a while. Every part of him—his shoulders, his hips, his legs— seemed terribly diminished, even his genitals, which looked small as a child's. He was pale, almost a glowing white. He turned his back to me and I put a drop of shampoo into my palm and soaped his head, where there were a few spidery remains of hair. It had not grown back this time, and the scalp was scaly and tough.

Something about the whole thing struck him as funny. "Just like old times," he said, and, though he no longer had enough wind to laugh, he turned and caught my hand and held it still long enough to lean over and give me a weak, wet kiss.

He smelled sweet when he stepped back out into the room and I toweled him down and held his pajama bottoms for him and he put his hands on my shoulders, steadying himself so he could get into them without falling over.

It made him feel better, the bathing, and when he got back into bed he slid down under the quilt and closed his eyes. The sun had not yet set, but the last rays were filtering through the pale curtains. He gave a small smile, in the most utterly peaceful way, and he said, "Another beautiful day with my Bear."

Monday, the real holiday, was another of those gorgeous days, the kind that cannot help but make you feel good. There were visitors all day long. His parents, his sisters Susan and Carol, and even Donald came in the afternoon. Many others, too. There was a veritable procession of family and friends, I guess because it was a holiday, and a beautiful day too, people were out, driving around.

In his shop at the barn, Paul had one job left from his work the past winter. An arched trellis for a formal garden he'd made for the O'Neils, summer people I hoped would be coming out from Cambridge that weekend. Friday evening I called them and they said their son would come over and get the trellis, but the weekend was drawing to a close and he hadn't called or come. For supper I made fresh pasta and salad and Paul had eaten a good big dish of it, sitting on the edge of our bed. When he was finished, I told him I was going over to Bide-a-wee to mow the lawn and then to the O'Neils to deliver the trellis. Earlier, he had made out a bill for it and put it in an envelope, addressing the outside in pencil.

I went first to Bide-a-wee, carrying the lawn mower from the house in the back of Paul's truck. No one was there. The lawn had not been mowed yet that spring. The grass was above my ankles, so it was slow going, pushing and then backing up over the clots of clippings. The feelings at Bide-a-wee are so strong, still, of Paul, of us. It is where we finally took hold of our love, and the peacefulness there will always be like lying in his arms. The little house, the patches of lawn and the gardens. The rose he bought for me the summer after we married was beginning to climb again on the old lobster-trap trellis he made for it. The yellow iris we planted at the top of the driveway were beginning to bloom. Pushing the mower, I circled round and round the lawn, feeling that love from him all over again.

When I was done, I shut off the mower and listened once again to the quiet. The staccato sound of a woodpecker rang out and a breeze made the new leaves come alive. I imagined Paul's truck lumbering down the drive, the horn gently blowing in announcement of his arrival. I saw him get out and lean down and take Gorm's head in his hands. I felt his arms close around me.

I left the mower there and went up to the barn to get the trellis. It wasn't as heavy as I had imagined, since he had made it pegged together in three sections, and I carefully loaded it, one section at a time, into the back of the truck. I had never been to the O'Neils, but on a drive not long ago we had chanced upon it, a big place with acres of green lawns, gardens everywhere, and a house that looked like the summer home of a president or some foreign dignitary.

Typical of Paul, he had never mentioned that these people, for whom he'd done several jobs, lived in such a house.

I found my way back there, a dirt road off another dirt road. There was a Mercedes in the driveway and the doors were open, lights on against the early part of the evening's darkness. Toe-tapping clarinet music was playing from somewhere in the house. I knocked on the door, ever louder, but roused no one. I went to all of the doors—there were many and it was hard to know which one they used. The place was wide open, but no one answered my knock. Finally I left the trellis at the kitchen door, wedging Paul's bill into the screen, and drove back home. It was almost dark.

I went upstairs. Paul was lying on his side in the bed, his eyes wide open. The woolen hat that he'd worn day and night for months and months had slipped off his head and lay beside him on the pillow. He struggled to sit up when he saw me, grimacing with the pain of the effort. "Hi, H," he said. Oxygen hissed into his nostrils. I sat down next to him and kissed his head. He still smelled sweet from the shampoo. I told him I'd mowed the lawn and delivered the trellis and he seemed pleased, but then he said, "I don't like you to have to do all those things for me."

"Well," I said, "it's done. Those things have been hanging over our heads for a while. Everything's out of the barn now. And you'll have some money coming in. Isn't that good?"

He took my hand and held it in both of his. "Yup," he said, "that is good."

I felt hot and sweaty from the work. "How about some sherbet?" I asked him.

"That sounds good," he said.

I went down to the kitchen and filled two bowls with orange sherbet and stuck gingersnaps on the side. I thought his breathing seemed better. I almost felt like calling our beloved hospice nurse, Genevieve, to tell her not to bother to come. If it had been anyone else I might have, but we had become so fond of her. She had a goodness that seemed to come out of the air toward us. I took the sherbet up on a tray and he lay on his back against the pillow. This time he didn't get up, but spooned the ice into his mouth from where he lay, his eyes shut as he ate. "I love you, H," he said.

I said, "I know. I love you too."

"I keep saying that, over and over. I feel like a broken record," he said.

"I know, me too. But it's true. You do love me, and I love you. You're my best love, Bear."

"Mmmm," he said, his eyes still shut.

Genevieve arrived soon after that. She let herself in and came upstairs and sat cross-legged on the floor beside the bed and talked with Paul. He told her about our trip to Washington and I shuddered, remembering how scared I had been every single minute, remembering how afraid I had been that he would die before we got home. And three months had passed since then. He told her how we climbed the pass on snowmobiles. "I'd always dreamed of going out west. It was the most beautiful place I've ever been," he said. He closed his eyes and lay quiet for a while. Genevieve sat still, almost in meditation.

At last he opened his eyes and turned to her. "What is it like to die?" he asked her.

"I don't know," she answered in her calm, reassuring voice, tinted with the accent of her native France, "but I know that beyond it there is peace."

"You have seen that?" he asked. He knew where her hospice work had taken her.

"Yes," she said. "I have seen that."

Paul began to nod, his head slack on the pillow. Genevieve pushed the button on the pump and there was a smooth rushing sound as more of the drug went into him. I got into my red nightshirt and lay down beside him. He was asleep and Genevieve went into her bedroom next door. We said good night, through the walls.

I turned out the light. It was around eleven. Paul was on his side, facing away from me, which is how he had been sleeping for months. Because of the position of the tumors in his lungs, it was the only comfortable way for him. I carefully put my arm around his waist and pulled in next to him. He took two deep breaths and then stopped, for too long a time. I sat up on my elbow and gently pushed him and he took in a great breath, several, and then stopped again. I waited and then leaned against him a little. He gulped in more air.

I got up and went to the door and called for Genevieve. She came in. Paul was awake, his eyes big. She crouched beside the bed and took his hand. She watched him. The breathing became louder and more uneven.

"Can you hear me, Paul?" she asked softly, and he nodded. She reached under the covers and felt his feet and then his hands. He was breathing in gulps.

"I think this may be it," she said to me, in a whisper. "Would you like to call anyone to be here with you?" I couldn't think of anyone—the last thing I wanted, really, was anyone there. For one thing, I didn't believe that she was right. I felt that this was just another one of his spells, that he'd catch his balance as he had often done before. For another thing, if ever there was something that was just between me and Paul, this was it.

"How about your minister?"

I thought a minute. Herb had been replaced by yet another new minister, this one named Dick. We didn't know Dick very well. I felt conflicted. If there was ever a time when I wanted to be alone with Paul, it was now. We had taken most of this long journey together. It seemed only right that we should take this last step alone. But Genevieve was already there. And she would stay, I knew. She asked me again: did I want a minister to come? I had no idea—is a minister supposed to be present at the time of death? I knew Paul believed in his Bible, I knew the comfort it had brought him in his times of need. I went to the phone and called Dick. He did not sound as if I had wakened him. I told him Paul might not make it through the night. He said he was alone with his youngest son. "Do you want me to come?" he asked. "Yes, I do," I said. And he said he would be there.

I went back into the room, into the ruinous sounds of Paul's strangulation. I lay down against his back and gently rubbed his shoulders. "Come on, Bear, hang in there," I said. He turned restlessly in the bed as he groped for air. He turned on his back and put his arm around me weakly. His eyes were dark pools and they bored into mine. "I love you, H," he said, his voice a soft wind, as if blowing out candles. It was the last thing he said. What came next was like thunder from within him. I held on to him. He took in gasps of air and then let loose, expelling the air in booming shout-moans. And then he lay still for an eerily long time before taking in another shuddering gulp of air. In an effort almost like flight, he pushed up against the mattress with his hands and then shoved his face into the pillow. Genevieve and I wrestled with him to get him back on his side, to get his face out of the pillow. The sheep outside the window fell silent and Dune, under the bed, made no noise.

There was no holding back the tears anymore and my own sobs mixed with his agonizing efforts.

It didn't seem like very long before Dick bounded up the stairs, his Bible stuffed into the back pocket of his jeans. He came in and knelt beside Genevieve, taking Paul's other hand. I seem to remember that Genevieve told me I needed to tell Paul to let go. Maybe she hadn't, but I began to tell him—into his ear, for I no longer felt he was seeing through his open eyes—that it was okay to let go. "Let go, Bear, let go," I said between my own sobs. "You can go now, everything's been taken care of. We have done all we can do. Let go, Bear. It's okay to let go now." I remember Dick and Genevieve, holding on to his hands, saying things like that to him also, muted voices in the wind of his storm.

It wasn't until I saw his fingers go white that I realized that they were right, that he was indeed dying, dying now, not tomorrow, that these nearly four years were drawing to an end. Over that long time, I had gone in and out of the knowledge that he would die. The past months, I had known it more clearly than ever. Yet somehow I had never imagined *how* he would die. I never thought he would die so hard, suffocating for days and days. I never thought he would die in my arms, that I would watch the life drain out of him as I did that night. I guess I thought he would die in a hospital when I wasn't there, and that the news would come to me in a phone call, filtered information. Or maybe I never really thought that far—only imagining the dying as having to live without him, not seeing the dying as an act, like a birth, like a tremendous effort, like the passage that it is.

That is what happened. Life pulled away from him and he was still. The clock beside the bed read ten after one. Dick asked me if Paul had a favorite prayer and I realized in confusion that I had no idea. I opened Paul's prayerbook, which was lying on the table beside his bed. Dick reached over and held my hand and together we read the words, with Paul between us. We read the prayer that begins "I believe in one God the Father Almighty, Maker of heaven and earth," and ends, "And I look for the Resurrection of the dead: And the life of the world to come." We dropped our hands and I got up off the bed and went to the roof window. The night air had been silent. Suddenly I heard all the sheep bells ring. I felt as if I heard the sheep running, fleeing across the field.

I turned. Paul lay on the bed, a waxy figure. Dick and Genevieve left the room and I went back and sat next to Paul, took his pale white hand in mine and held it for what seemed like a long, long time. I knew at last that death was not the end. I can't say I saw a white mist or blinding flashes of light, but I knew that I had seen Paul leave his body, leave it before he died. I knew that the two realms of which I'd read so much had joined inside that room for a moment, long enough for me to witness the spirit separate from the body. And Paul's spirit was grander, more generous than any I'd ever known, any I'd ever imagined.

The oxygen continued to blow into his nose and the machine *ka-klunked* away in its own persistent rhythm at the foot of the stairs. Genevieve had to call Donna, since she, as a nurse, would be the only one who would be able to pronounce Paul dead. I didn't hear her drive in, she just appeared in the doorway and I could hear her and Genevieve going over Paul's vital signs, and then I heard one of them calling Dr. Liepman. After that, Genevieve went downstairs and turned off the machine. As soon as she did the onerous racket ended and as much as I hated that machine and its intrusive presence I felt an incredible emptiness when the noise stopped, as if Paul had died a second time.

I stood again by the window, looking out. Dick came over to me and put his hands on my shoulders. "He'll go straight to heaven," I said, "like a rocket."

"Like a rocket?" Dick sounded kind of incredulous. "Knowing Paul, I think he'll probably take his time."

We left him then, closing the door to the room and

going downstairs. I felt completely at a loss, like a character in an absurd play. There were visitors in our house. My husband's cold body lay on our bed upstairs. I didn't know what to do. I sensed they didn't either. They stood in a row in the kitchen, Donna, Genevieve, Dick, somber as soldiers in a foreign land. I said, "Would anyone like some tea?" and they all nodded, yes, yes, that sounds good. I felt their relief as I lit the blue flame under the kettle.

I heard tires on the gravel outside and I looked out into the blackness to see a hearse pull into the driveway. Who had called the hearse? I didn't know, but a tall, tanned, smiling young man came into the kitchen. He was dressed in a suit. His hair was perfect. It's the middle of the night, I thought. The absurd play continued. He held out his hand to me. He had the air of a salesman and I recoiled, walking backward to the chair by the table and sinking into it, suddenly aware I was still in my nightshirt. He introduced himself. The smile never left him. I heard him tell me to come to the funeral home in the morning and to bring a suit for Paul. And clean underwear. And shoes. He held out his hand again and left, smiling. I heard men's voices in the front hall and a commotion on the stairway.

These are the things that I never imagined, that strange men would come in the middle of the night and take Paul away. I did not see them but I heard their footfalls in the room overhead and then watched out the window as the red taillights of the long black car disappeared into the night.

Part Three

10

I don't know what happened when Paul died. He was just one man, an ordinary man who barely grazed the earth before he passed back out of it. The same could be said for most of us. He was not a hero. He had no fame and certainly no fortune. No monuments or legends are left by which to remember him. Or any of us. Most of our stories are private, dying when we do, carried on in the hearts of our children or those closest to us, if they are carried at all. That Paul was so desperately odd when I first knew him and that he grew into a man of such grace is something only I and a few others can bear witness to. What was his struggle all about? Was his illness and death the hardest of all?

It is always hard to make sense of the death of a young man. In Paul's case, I find it even harder. If our lives are truly here to grace the lives of others, then Paul honored that mission. He did struggle to overcome the towering adversities that faced him, but when he realized the battle was over, he gracefully accepted that end. I don't know how he knew so much about death. He seemed to have it balanced, just right, on the tip of his finger.

It wasn't until Paul died that I realized or even thought for the first time of how stupidly our society has encountered death. We hide it or we hide from it. Or we are asked to hide it. We carry it inside us like our worst secret. We all conspire to keep the secret, a conspiracy so complete it is hard to know whether we keep it because it is too hard to part with or because our words won't be heard.

As the days and weeks passed, the truth of this crystallized. I realized that up to that time I *knew* so little about death, I'd *heard* so little about death. I thought of it as a terrible truth we must all face and move past. But I knew no specifics, none at all.

We have distanced ourselves. The possibility of weaning ourselves away from our dead has been taken from us. Not that many years ago, families kept their dead in the house until the burial. My mother remembers her grandfather lying in their living room for several days after his death.

There was so much I learned from Paul's death, so much I wanted to tell. Right after he died, I climbed back into bed with him, held on to his hand for as long as I dared, for I knew that Dick and Genevieve lingered outside the door. I knew this might seem macabre, maybe even ghoulish, but the need to do it was great. Putting aside what I felt others might think, it seemed like the most natural thing to do. I later shared this with other widows, who said they had done the same thing, and it made me feel better to know this was their instinct, too. I also read that Buddhists sleep with their dead on the first night after their departure. Knowing this soothed me.

Though I had never thought about any of it, when it all happened the thing that felt the most unnatural was not that I had clung to his pale, cold hand and spoken to him as if he were still filled with life, but that his body was taken away so abruptly, as if it were something grotesque and awful, something to be hidden. Lying in bed one night, a couple of months after Paul died, it came to me that death is an unexplored intimacy. We know more about our feelings about our sex lives than we know about our feelings about death. There is certainly more of a forum for sex than there is for death.

Maybe that's how it should be. Sex, after all, is most often an expression of joy, an indulgence in pleasure, and this is not what death is. At best, death is a mystery, a passage to new life. At worst, it is the most painful part of life. At worst, it is the end. But Paul briefly opened the curtain of mystery for me and I saw death as much more than that. After he died I wanted to talk about it, I wanted to share what he had brought me. For in his life he brought me many, many gifts, but in his death he brought me something stronger, a joy in knowing the strength of his spirit, which lives on in me, so that I am never alone and never will be as long as I have him, so powerfully alive in me.

In our culture, just after a death, there is a great outpouring of sympathy. That was the way it was for me. There are the days following the death, then the funeral, then perhaps a few weeks. That is enough, isn't it? After that, it is over, for most everyone on the outside. We are urged by our family, by our friends, to put it all behind us and move on. And of course, that is the desire, the deep desire. Who does not want to go about their life with ease and a certain amount of contentment? I certainly did. And yet, this is truly a case where the intellect and the emotions fail to intersect.

Paul's death came to me as news. It came as good news. That was the surprise to me. Of course, it was not news. We had anticipated it and feared it and loathed it, but it came anyway, an apocalypse that upended my life in a way that I had not expected. And of course it was not good. It was good only in the way that I experienced it, the way that I perceived that death truly can be redemptive. The redemption was Paul's. That was the good news. Everything else about it was devastating.

Having had so much time to consider the possibility, I felt I was prepared. In the days after Paul's death, a kind of euphoria set in. There had been more than three years of struggle and then months of tension, night after night not knowing if he would die that night or the next. His death brought not only resolution to that terrible tension but an affirmation of the truth that I kept thinking couldn't be, that he would bear his death with grace.

Beginning just hours after his death, our house filled up with people, people talking about Paul. So many talked about his transformation, what a miracle it had been that he had grown from who he was when I met him to who he was when he died. One of Paul's many doctors wrote me a card, and in it he said that Paul was truly one of the most remarkable men he had ever met. Another man, the CEO of a successful company, came to visit me the day after Paul died. Paul had done carpentry work for him and they shared a great fondness for each other. He was a distinguished man, with powerful and influential friends all over the country, but that day he sat on our sofa, shook his head and said, "Paul was a magnificent man." It touched me in the most profound way to know that Paul had affected other people as he had me.

With all this to hold me, I even thought that perhaps I would not grieve, since we had grieved together as his death approached. We had had time to say good-bye, and the last thing he said was, "I love you." I felt that these were gifts that don't accompany all deaths and that these things alone would fuel me past grieving. I was wrong. At every juncture, I was wrong.

There is no shortage of books on this topic and I read them all. And some of them are good, very good, but they could not really tell me about me, tell me about Paul, and they could not bring him back. Which is what I wanted. That's all I wanted, even knowing how illogical it was.

Sometimes when I talk about Paul's death to people I don't know very well, I tell them about Dune. It may be I am trying to tell them about me in a way that might put them at ease. Or I may be trying to tell them how far-reaching grief is, how longlasting it can be, even for a dog.

On the night that Paul died, after the men from the funeral home had left, I suddenly thought, "Where is Dune?" The last I had known, she had been under our bed, her customary place to sleep. With a surge of dread, I realized that strange men had come into our bedroom. She had never barked. The front door had been left open for some time, as the men came and went. Our door is just a few feet from a busy road. She must have gone outside. Still in my nightshirt, I ran out, calling her, imagining she had run off in confusion or worse, that she had been run over. In the darkness, I called and called. "Dune! Dune!"

In spite of the springlike warmth in the air, the earth was still cold under my bare feet. I went back inside, still calling. I climbed the stairs. If I hadn't been frantic to find Dune I am not sure how long it would have been before I went back in that room. I got down on my knees and lifted the quilt to see under the bed. She was lying down, her front legs stretched straight in front of her, her head up and alert but her eyes glassy and distant. "Oh, Dune, for Christ's sake, *there* you are," I said. I reached under and put my finger through her collar. "Come on out, come on." I pulled gently. She was like a dead weight and her eyes didn't move. I tugged again. "Dune?" No response. I let go of her collar and patted the rug. "Come *on*, Dune. Come on out."

When she was a puppy she was run over. No bones were broken but she went into shock, lying still as a stone, her eyes open but unfocused. The vet had said, "Give her a few days. She'll come out of it." That was what this reminded me of. I hated to leave her there but as hard as I found it to believe, it felt as if she too needed to work this out. Or maybe she was keeping watch. I left her with those mysteries. She stayed there until the next day, when she quietly emerged.

Even before Paul died, she had started to come apart, occasionally peeing on the rugs or pooping next to the toilet upstairs. After he died, she lost control of herself completely. I finally took up all the rugs that would come up and tried leaving her in the linoleum-floored back hall at night, going to bed without her. But she would whimper pitifully like a puppy and I'd relent and let her upstairs. She still provided that great sought-for commodity, suddenly torn from my life: love. At night she leapt up onto the bed and nuzzled under my arm, and when I opened my eyes in the mornings she wagged her tail brightly and yip-yipped excitement over a new day. I clung to her and to her presence in the house, trying to overlook the messes she left everywhere.

She also turned vicious toward anyone who attempted to enter our solitary home. She snarled and lunged at guests when they came to the door. Nothing I could say or do would stop her.

This went on for months and months and I began to disbelieve that her tiresome behavior was in any way connected with Paul's death. I could hardly remember her as a mannered dog. It all just became an added burden.

But at times I wondered if she were mirroring my feelings. Was I leaving messes everywhere? Did I snarl and lunge? At moments, I could see this allegory as real.

There was one other incident that involved Dune: Paul used to take Dune to work with him in his truck. It was their daily routine. After Paul stuck his oatmeal dish in the sink, she waited by the back door. Any indication of his possible departure—lacing up his boots, reaching for his coat, pulling on his hat—precipitated leaps and yelps. If she wasn't with him, she could hear the sound of his truck from a great distance and I could often tell that he was coming, long before he arrived, when she would suddenly get up and put her nose next to the door and give a small whine.

His truck stayed where I had parked it the evening he died, after I got back from delivering the trellis. The battery went dead. The next spring, nearly a year after his death, old friends came to visit for the weekend. They arrived in John's truck. John is a farmer, and also sells farm equipment in Vermont. Toward the end of the weekend I ventured, "John, do you think we could get Paul's truck started?" I was sensitive about asking men to help me with things that needed doing and chose the favors carefully.

"No problem," he said. "Have you got cables?"

I knew Paul kept jumper cables in the shed. We went down and rummaged around, moving aside bushel baskets and cases of oil and the orange chain saw and all its para-phernalia, looking for these lifelines that Paul always kept handy. Dune sniffed around in the corners as we moved and rearranged. We finally spotted the yellow cord of the cables under a tangle of baling twine.

John nosed his truck up against the bumper of Paul's and we opened the hoods. Dune sat near the trucks, oddly still. I got up into the seat, waiting for John to give me the signal. The inside of the cab still smelled like sawdust. On the dashboard was a yellow Post-it note in Paul's handwriting, a list of nails he needed for some long-ago completed job. I pumped the gas pedal. John stuck his thumb up and I threw out the clutch and turned the key. The truck came alive with a great roar as I pressed down on the gas. Black smoke poured from the tailpipe. Above the noise of the engine I heard Dune. I jumped down from behind the wheel. She was racing in great wide circles around the truck, a hysterical blur of white, rushing around and around and around. I knew at once that for Dune the sound of the engine meant only one thing: Paul was back. We all stood and watched her, no one doubting what she felt.

And so I tell these stories because it is easier to tell about a dog. They are curious and seem to put people at ease. They deflect the attention from me. If Dune were telling the stories, I wonder what she would choose to tell. I like to think that I handled it all just right, with balance and grace, and that none of the seams ever showed in the hastily stitched costume I wore. But of course that isn't true.

The morning after they took Paul away, I went down to the funeral home. The man had told me to bring a suit for

Paul and I'd thought about that. There was the suit he'd
bought for our wedding. It was the only suit he ever
owned and that was the only time he wore it. It was hanging in our closet, the vest buttoned beneath the jacket. A
suit? I asked myself, hearing that man's middle-of-the-
night instructions in my head once again. I went upstairs to
the bedroom. It felt like a cavern, a huge tomb. From the
bottom drawer of Paul's bureau I took a pair of jeans, leaving the red kerchief in the back pocket where he'd put it
the last time he'd worn them. Because he wore them a lot,
he had three red-and-black-checked flannel shirts. I chose
the nicest one. I pressed it to my face and breathed in all the
peculiar odors of Paul, the sawdust, the sweat, the sweet
aftershave. On the floor of the closet were his green leather
boots, the toes worn from all the kneeling he did in his
work. From the top drawer I took socks and clean underwear, as the man had asked. I took these in my arms and
went downstairs. His brown-duck work jacket hung from
a hook in the back hall, his blue cap hung over it. I took
both and set everything down on the kitchen counter. To
lay Paul to rest was to dress him as he was. What else? I
stood thinking, closing my eyes, imagining him moving
about in his shop or sitting behind the wheel of his truck.
At last I went out to his workbench and dug around in his
toolbox. He had a lot of different hammers, but I knew the
one I was looking for, the one he had had since he was
fourteen. The handle was darker than the others, the grain
worn smooth as stone. I gathered all this into the car and
drove to the funeral home, which occupied an old Victorian house.

A lugubrious young man who looked like he'd just come from the tanning salon greeted me and ushered me inside. He took the small stack of clothing from my arms, balancing the hammer and the boots on top. He glanced briefly at them and then back at me.

"Paul was a carpenter," I said, feeling a little defensive.

"Yes," he said, smiling politely.

In the parlor, he offered me a silken chair. New Age music oozed from a boom box on the desk. He sat near me on a brocade couch, crossed his slender legs and asked questions about Paul—where was he born, how old was he, what did he do for a living and how did he die—and wrote my answers onto a clipboard.

When he was through with the questions, he took me upstairs. The place was still laid out like a house. A small room, obviously once a bedroom, was crowded with caskets of all varieties—oak and metal and mahogany. The lids were open, revealing the linings of crepe and silk, all soft colors, light blues, beiges, violets. They all looked the same to me: inappropriate for Paul. Each had little cream-colored cards on top, the price neatly hand-lettered. $1,600. $3,200. $5,000. He told me that there were others too, one made of particle board, another of plywood, but he had none of those available to show me. They would be much cheaper, he pointed out.

I wanted to flee. Without even making a rough calculation in my head, I made the choices rapidly: an oak box, a cement liner, no calling hours, closed casket, no flowers, please. Funeral on Saturday, in the little Chesham church where we had been married five years before.

When I got home, even more people had arrived. My sister had flown in from Seattle, and my aunt and uncle were there. Friends had come from everywhere, it seemed. One of Paul's sisters arrived, and then his parents came. There was a great deal of solace in that. There was a lot going on in the kitchen. I could hardly get into the room. I felt people hugging me and I heard myself talking. My sister and some others were making lunch for the crowd that was gathering.

I left them and went to my office. I pulled up a new file onto the screen of my computer and began to write Paul's obituary. I started out, "Paul Douglas Bolton, 39, of Chesham, New Hampshire, died this morning after a long battle with cancer." I stopped and mentally continued, realizing there wasn't much to say, not in the way that I wanted to, not in the way the newspapers would have it. His education was simple, his vocation humble and without accolades. There were no offspring and his survivors were limited. So few paragraphs to sum up a life that had brought me so much. I sat and stared at the screen, trying to think of what else I could say. I could think of nothing else and printed it out.

The night before the funeral I had stayed up late with my sister, Paul's sister, Susan, and a friend, Annie. I sorted through boxes of photographs, finding ones I liked of Paul. I wanted to have pictures of him at his funeral.

I came across one I had taken when I first knew him in 1978. I studied the photograph as if seeing the dark withdrawn man in the baggy work clothes for the first time. It was hard to imagine that he was the same Paul who awed me with his strength and his bravery as he approached death. In the intervening days I had heard people speak of his saintliness and ministers say they felt in him a Divine Presence, but I never heard anyone say that about him back then. Quite the contrary. I remembered once more our neighbor of long ago saying, "Paul Bolton, he's a nutcase, isn't he?" I recalled the psychologist, Max, saying, "Edie, if you see something in Paul, I'm sure you're the only one who ever has or ever will." And I remembered Paul, up in his attic room, putting his arms around me and saying, "Please don't feel sorry for me." I stared at the photograph and realized that peace can come into a life of misery, that love can truly make a difference.

We arranged the photos we liked best on a big poster board, starting with those earlier pictures and going all the way up to one taken a couple of months before he died. It is in front of me as I write. When the photo was taken, he knew he was going to die. He had five tumors in his brain, tumors crowded his already greatly diminished lungs. In fact by then the disease had invaded nearly every part of him. Yet this is not the face of a dying man. His expression is open, his gaze strong and full of courage, his Mona Lisa smile wise. We worked until very late that night, creating a collage of Paul that seemed to document his transfiguration.

Early the next morning, I wedged the board into the back of my car and took it to the empty church. It was damp and cold inside. The little building is not used during

the winter and the heat had not yet been turned on. I set
the board on the easel in the foyer, where they post an-
nouncements, and stood back. I was pleased with the way
it looked. I pushed open the door to the sanctuary. Inside,
it was still and quiet. On tiptoe, I went in. The old wooden
floors creaked. I sat down in the last pew, where Paul and I
most often sat during worship. The just-rising sun was filtering through the colored glass windows. Squares of yellow and purple light glanced off the faded carpet in the
aisle. This little church had brought us so much. I thought
about our wedding day and the excitement that swirled
around us then. I replayed it in my mind and I remembered
the little things, too, how, just minutes before the ceremony, Mary Upton had taken a comb from her purse and
run it through the back of Paul's hair, saying, "You boys,
you always forget." I thought of our weekly attendance
there and remembered the way Paul used to take up the
collection, holding his tie against his chest with one hand
and stretching his long arm to reach Millie Greenwood,
who always sat alone in the middle of the pew. I thought
about the first time we had come to this church, before we
were married, remembering Mary Upton's sermon on
love. *Love bears all things, believes all things, hopes all things,
endures all things. . . . Love never ends; as for prophecy, it will
pass away; as for tongues, they will cease; as for knowledge, it will
pass away.* I heard the words in my head as if she were
speaking them at that moment. But I heard the message
very differently. I knew then better than at any time in my
life how quickly good things can pass away. I hoped against

all hope that love never ends. In the cold stillness, I felt Paul's warmth next to me, felt his hand take hold of mine.

The day grew bright and sunny and warm. Perhaps because of Paul's long suffering, his long ordeal, the day of his funeral became a celebration. It could have been mistaken for a party. Cars lined the road and the house brimmed with friends and family, spilling out onto the lawn in the new summer warmth. There was barely room inside the little church. I felt elated. I knew that Paul's long trials were over and that he had redeemed himself through his death by his dignity and his grace, by the faith he had in God. His suffering was over. Those who loved him were here, with me, and through this ceremony I felt a needed sense of closure. We sang hymns—"There's a Wideness in God's Mercy" and "For All the Saints." Dick spoke of Paul as a quiet, private and happy man. He said how one woman in town had told him that Paul was the nicest man she had ever known. He spoke of Paul's humility and of his good humor, his grace. He spoke of his work as a carpenter, how he constantly brought new life to the homes around him, and he spoke of how Paul had resurrected the barn, even when he was so sick. He ended his comments this way: "Paul was not a stoic but he was one who carried his burdens with much dignity. In the gospel lesson this morning, Jesus speaks of going to prepare a room for his followers. In his lifetime, Paul prepared many a room for the good comfort of others. During the last months of his life, friends and family members gathered around him and prepared a room in which he could find comfort and release from the pain of his cancer. As hard as it was for him to have other people preparing a room for him in his last days, when the work was done he graciously received this gift. The room was sunny and the warm rays of the sun fell upon him in his bed. A mobile of wooden boats hung directly over his bed, making their ways on the currents of air. And through the window he could hear tinkling of the bells hanging on the necks of the sheep in his field. On the last day of his life, Edie delivered his last project, a trellis upon which roses would grow. His work was done. He could go home. . . ."

When the service was over, Paul's friend Harvey played the fiddle in the back of the church, some of the same tunes he had played for our wedding. Tears streamed down his face as he played.

A long, long, long line of cars followed the sleek black hearse from the church, around the corner, past the depot, down the narrow back road to the little cemetery in the woods. As I rode I looked behind me at the snake of cars that followed us. Paul and I had so often walked on this road, where the pavement was broken and grass grew up from the cracks. The road is barely passable by two cars at once. I thought how odd this must look. As we passed the field filled with the sheep Paul had fed all winter, several of them bleated. Coincidence, I suppose, but on this bright warm third day of June, I chose to believe they were saying good-bye to their friend.

Some people walked from the church, and a friend went back to the house and put Dune on the leash and walked with her up to the cemetery.

It is a long slope up to Paul's grave. People scattered all along the way, many crowded around the grave and joined hands. Together we sang "Amazing Grace" as the men in dark suits lowered the casket into the earth.

The silence that followed was what I hadn't expected. People remembered me for a few weeks, and I was grateful for that. There are some, of course, who still remember me, bless them. But it is a long empty road that lies ahead after that, with so much to fill. No matter how many friends, no matter how much caring, no matter how well intended, it cannot replace what is gone, which was half of my self, half of me.

Nearly everything sparked a desire for Paul. Hot knives of memory sank in, day after day. I found myself wandering from room to room, looking out the window toward the driveway, as if I were expecting someone. I'd catch myself, and realize I was waiting for him to return. The pain increased, it seemed, rather than eased. People said, "Time will heal all," and they meant well, but as time passed I experienced something like the opposite. I was beset with an odd fear, a kind of panicky feeling that the more time that elapsed, the more distance there was between me and the last time I'd held Paul's hand, the last time I'd looked into his eyes.

I left his watch on his bedside table for months after he died, the second hand still sweeping round and round. I left untouched the pocketknife and the little assortment of things he'd taken from his pants pocket the last time he'd undressed. Perhaps this made it seem as if less time had elapsed. Who knows? I can't say why I did it. Eventually I took all these treasures, plus many others, and set them in a pine chest, but until then leaving them as he'd left them helped me.

I had loneliness but I also had solitude. I wasn't sure, sometimes, how to distinguish one from the other. I know that the loneliness hurt but the solitude offered me contemplation, a chance to sort it all out, to try to make sense of it all.

I did a lot of things to try to take the hurt away. I fasted. I walked for miles and miles and miles. I talked with other widows. So often, they expressed anger. If I felt anger, I could not find it. How could I be angry at Paul for dying? He had tried so hard to live. And he devoted his final months to making me a place, and he did everything he could, even in his final weakness, to make that place complete.

If I felt anger, it was toward his family. They had hurt him throughout his life and when he fell ill, they were, for the most part, absent. I couldn't understand it. It is even more perplexing for me to have to report that now, nearly three years after Paul's death, I love them. I think of them as family, and at holidays, we gather. I cannot look at Arthur without conjuring the bittersweet memory of those early days when he and Paul shared a home. With each of his sisters, I have taken vacation and traveled to distant places. On summer Sunday afternoons, I sometimes join Elizabeth and Arthur at local organ concerts. Occasionally, Elizabeth is the featured musician and I admire her skill.

They rarely mention Paul, or his passing. The meaning of his struggle, or that he struggled at all, is never acknowledged. The meaning of his life, not even the essence of his life, has never been broached. In many ways it is as if he never existed. Perhaps there's a hurt and confusion so deep they cannot find words. I cannot explain why I have warmed to them, except that there is a residue in each of them that reminds me of Paul—the way his brother butters his bread, the way his father folds his arms, the color of his sister's eyes. I will never understand the way they treated Paul, but I know that Paul forgave it, which, after a great struggle in my heart, I realized was good enough for me.

Slowly, like a haze, the summer passed. I thought that the gravestone would be the last thing I could do for Paul, the final gift. Getting it into the ground took well over a year. The following spring, on Memorial Day, I planted a flower garden at the grave, to observe the day he died. Red geraniums, white and blue trumpets of petunias, blue bachelor's buttons, white alyssum—all bloomed brightly, with only a little tending on my part.

The grave had become a place for me, I might even say a sacred place, except that it was freewheeling. I sat there in prayer, but I also picnicked there with friends. It is only a short distance from the house. There are no buildings nearby, only a wide and colorful wetland where beavers live and work and great blue herons graze, a marsh Paul and I often walked beside.

Since Paul's death, Dune and I have been to the cemetery countless times. As soon as we get to the bottom of the hill, I let her off the leash and she charges upward like an arrow toward the grave. I follow, up the long hill.

Paul's plot is in front, the last one in. Dune runs in ragged circles as I get nearer. She does this without fail. The hill is south-facing and on warm spring days and in the fall I often sit there, feeling the warmth of the sun. When friends or family come, I like to walk them to the cemetery, surprise them with the life that abounds around the grave.

I have brought things there, for Paul. I feel like a member of a primitive culture bringing amulets and talismans. There are stones that I've laid in a collar around the marker, some that he once scooped up off a beach or pocketed from the top of a peak we'd reached. We used to keep these stones, most of them smooth and oddly colored, on the hearth beside the stove. After he died, I looked at them and considered putting them out in the woods. But then, instead, I took them to the grave.

After that, I brought stones back from wherever I'd been. I walked the beaches on the island of St. John, head down, looking for shells and stones. I collected a basketful of shells, their insides pink and purple, polished by sun and water. I was hoping that I would find a piece of coral worn by the tide into the shape of a cross. While I was there, I had seen one on someone's mantel. It seemed like the perfect thing to carry back to Paul. I looked and looked. On the last day, I spotted a small piece of coral smoothed into the shape of a heart. Elated, I picked it up and held its smoothness. I felt as if I'd found a four-leaf clover. I don't know how or why this happens, but I've experienced it before; perhaps it's the power of suggestion. Within the next three hours I found three more pieces shaped like hearts. I brought these back in my suitcase, carrying the basket of shells separately through customs. The shells I put beside the marker and the heart-shaped coral I pressed into the earth in front of the bachelor's buttons.

From Wales I brought a squarish stone that fit snugly in my palm. It was deep red, from the sand flats below Dylan Thomas's boathouse. In Scotland, I walked through a fine mist on the beach at Findhorn, picking up stones to bring home. There was no sand on this beach, just the stones, all browns and reds and grays, and almost all oval, a wonderful symmetry of size and color. When the waves came in against these stones, there was a happy sound, like laughter, as the water sucked back out to sea. As had happened on St. John, I found one in the shape of a heart. My eyes just fell on it, drawn like magnets. This time there was only one. It was big and gray and smooth and I brought it home to the grave and placed it in front, among the other stones.

All the while I had been thinking about the gravestone, working on it in my mind's eye. Because it was to be the last gift, I wanted it to be perfect. And of course, if I want something to be perfect, it cannot be, so my head went round and round with the possibilities, never able to take hold of the reality, because whatever it will be, it won't be perfect.

I did not want one of those "Rock of Ages" monuments. They are ordinary and almost offensive to me in their sameness. I knew that there were alternatives. At first I felt I wanted a marker such as that which marks Archibald MacLeish's grave—a big round boulder with just the name MACLEISH carved into the roughness. I thought that suited Paul. Simple, and of the earth. I wanted to find the stone on our land, maybe from one of our old walls. I spent quite a bit of time looking everywhere for the right stone. I found one across the field, back by the river. It was granite, dark gray with moss. I climbed up and sat on it. It was comfortable, which was important. I imagined I would like it as a place to sit. But then, practicalities set in: how could I get this boulder out of the woods? How would I transport it to be inscribed? I began to think about other kinds of stones.

Several years ago I wrote an article about modern grave robbers, antique dealers who were taking the beautiful old slate stones out of cemeteries and selling them as folk art in galleries in New York City for thousands of dollars. After the story came out, a man named Casimer Michalczyk sent me a letter, handwritten in elegant script. Included in the envelope were a sheaf of photographs and a couple of newspaper clippings. He claimed to be one of only two left who could carve these slate gravestones. The stones in the pictures he sent me were shaped like the old ones, with rounded tops and shoulders and names carved in Old-English lettering. Angels in ellipses ornamented the tops and vines were etched in around the edges. I told him I would put him in my files for a possible future story. I meant it, but I forgot about him almost as soon as I'd tucked his letter into my file drawer. Thinking now, I remembered him.

Paul loved slate. He worked with it on roofs and when he found a slate with just the right run of grain, he saved it. I have one of these, so big I can hardly believe it was a single roofing slate. I use it for a table top. And of course Paul admired the work of all fine craftsmen. The pictures and the articles in my files suggested this man was an artist. I remembered that the stones were beautiful, but perhaps most of all I remembered that they were expressive. His stones carried verses and pictures that represented the person being memorialized. For a woman who loved birds, he had carved birds in flight around her name. For a man who loved to sail, he'd carved a graceful sloop, sails filled, puffy clouds passing overhead.

Casimer Michalczyk's studio was on Martha's Vineyard. I called him and told him the reason for my interest. He invited me to his studio. It was October when I finally went. Casimer is a short man, a small man, with a bristly gray mustache and narrow fox-brown eyes that move about quickly. His voice has a melancholy tone, as if everything throughout his life had been touched with sadness. He showed me some of the stones he had made, smooth, carefully crafted monuments, each cut with hand tools.

Though I had intended to, I didn't write him as soon as I got home. I kept putting it off, mystified by my own procrastination. I can only guess that writing the letter would finalize the project. I knew that between the time I wrote the letter and the time when the stone would be delivered there would be as many as six or eight months. Casimer has a waiting list, and he carves one stone at a time. Each one takes him six or eight weeks. Even so, I waffled. I suddenly thought that slate would be a bad choice. It splits and chips, and I felt the stone could be damaged easily. One night it even struck me that the carver was too old to do this, and that he might die before the stone was finished. Many things came to mind, all representing nothing more than delay, but as each consideration came up, it seemed real and worth thinking over.

I have a file now that is at least two inches thick, filled with letters from Casimer in his lovely archaic handwriting. We wrote back and forth like old friends, and when he finally wrote to tell me that he was going to start on Paul's stone I was almost startled. I had been lulled into his pace. Almost eight months had passed, and as I looked at the calendar I knew I did not need to delay any longer. I was beginning to get anxious that another winter would go by without a permanent marker on the grave.

Several nights I lay awake. Casimer had asked for the inscription I would like to have on the stone. I wrote a poem and then discarded it. This was going to be permanent and it had to epitomize everything that was Paul. The poem was eighteen lines long. At fifty cents a letter, it would cost an extra thousand dollars. What I wanted was for someone to come along, a stranger, and read the stone. From that alone I hoped they would know as much as could be known about Paul from so few words, so little space. I found myself sitting at my desk playing with words, moving them around. I wanted the word *grace*. I wanted the word *love*. I wanted the word *gentle*.

And what about an ornament? Casimer was a fine enough artist to have been able to carve a portrait of Paul, but that seemed too risky. While I knew he was capable of making a likeness, I doubted he could capture the tiny things so special to me about Paul. That would be too much to ask of any artist. I thought about the tools of Paul's trade, a hammer and plane, but that seemed too predictable. Then I thought about Bide-a-wee, the little house, our home. It was the most special thing that we shared. It had come back to life along with us. Finally, Casimer called. He said that if I wanted the stone done by the fall, he would have to have all the information as soon as possible.

That was it. A deadline.

I sketched the design on a piece of paper and mailed it to him. I went over to Bide-a-wee and took pictures. There was snow on the ground and the trees were stark behind it. It would have to be good enough.

The design evolved from there. Casimer sent me six sketches, playing around with the words and the spacing and with borders and styles. I chose two and sent them back, saying I wanted a blend of the two. It seemed as if by return mail he sent a blueprint—it was full size, the size of the stone, three feet high and almost two feet across—with the design as it would be on the stone.

The lettering was beautiful, exact, like the letters of the alphabet that were strung up over the blackboard in my early grade-school classes. I checked over the words for the spelling. Letter by letter I read over the message I had sent to Casimer to carve on the slate. At the top, over the carving of the house, I drew in a heart. I thought it might seem sentimental, but hearts meant something to Paul. Sometimes I would draw one and leave it on his breakfast plate. I sent him one once when he was in the hospital, a big paper cutout of a heart reddened with a thick marker, and he pinned it to the bulletin board near his bed, next to the multitude of snapshots he kept tacked up to remind him of home. It made him smile. He took it for what it was: a sign of love. I added another one at the bottom of the blueprint, and drew in lilies around the foundation of the house. They hadn't shown in the wintry pictures I'd sent Casimer.

I sent it back, this time including a check for $450, another installment on what would be a total of $2,000. I considered that an incredible bargain for the work of art he would be creating for me. I told him that sometime I would like to come out to the Vineyard and see him at work on the stone. We exchanged more letters. At last, I made reservations on the ferry. About a week beforehand, he called. His tone was worried and anxious. He wouldn't be on the island on the fourteenth after all. I didn't know what to think, but somehow I imagined that he must be behind in his work and was making excuses to keep me from seeing he hadn't made much progress. I didn't mind. I was beginning to want to slow this process down. I tried to let him know it was okay with me. I would come another time. I wanted him to believe me because I really felt almost relieved that I didn't have to go.

On Labor Day, my friend Jamie invited me to the Vineyard for the weekend. It was a beautiful blue-sky day, such as many we'd had during that most glorious of summers. Jamie was at the landing, waiting to meet me. When I got off the boat, I suggested we walk over to Casimer's and see if he was there. He was not supposed to be, according to the itinerary he had sent me. All summer long he had sent me his schedules, when he would be on the island, when he would be in Connecticut. We walked up through Oak Bluffs, which was bursting with the activities of this final summer weekend.

When we got to Casimer's shop, I peaked in through the screen door. He was there, bent over a stone. I knocked. He looked up, startled. I felt suddenly timid. I really hadn't thought he'd be there, wanted only to see if I could spot Paul's stone somewhere inside. I shouldn't have come unannounced. If he hadn't made much progress on the stone, this could embarrass him.

"Hello!" he said and unhooked the screen door from the inside so we could come in. My eyes adjusted to the darker light. I was trying to apologize for coming unexpectedly, but at the same time I could see that the stone he had been working on, in front of us now on the table, was Paul's. And it was almost finished. He had all the letters carved. He was working on the carving of the house. He took his rough hand and swept the slate dust away.

"What do you think?" he asked.

I was overcome. Though I had seen almost every stone he had ever carved, during our tours of the cemeteries, this seemed infinitely more beautiful. "It's very beautiful," was all I could muster.

"I'm working on those lilies," he said. Around the

foundation of the little house, he was coaxing blooms up out of the stone. He wanted me to tell him if the trees looked right. In the photos I had sent, there were no leaves on the trees, and he wasn't sure just how they looked in the summer. Were the tops full and balanced or did they hang down? He had several sketches of trees tacked to the wall, and he asked me if any of them looked right. I picked one that was sort of close. I said that the trees at Bide-a-wee leaned over the house in a protective way. He nodded. "Yes, yes, all right," he said.

The one important thing he wanted me to decide was whether I wanted the stone shipped or whether I wanted to come to pick it up. He seemed to want me to have it shipped, I guessed because that way it would be covered by insurance. The ride on the ferry can be extremely rough sometimes. I have seen cars tossed against each other. Not long ago a garbage truck, full and returning to the mainland to unburden itself, toppled over onto a small car, flattening it on the deck. The rides are like the weather: you take your chances. But I liked the idea of coming to get it, in Paul's truck. The drawback was that I would need to have help. The stone weighs 300 pounds and Casimer and I could not load it alone. I told him that if I could find a helper I would come to get it.

I see now how helpless we are in what we can do for the people we have lost. To make our hearts ache a little less, we cry and we talk and talk and talk. We write poems. We erect monuments. We carry their belongings. After I glimpsed the stone in the dim light of Casimer's studio on that last Labor Day trip to the Vineyard, I was beset with melancholia. I supposed it had to do with the finishing of the stone, so final. It was what I wanted. It was as special as I could make it, but it didn't seem adequate. Nothing seemed adequate. It also meant, in some important way, that I had to get on with my life.

In the days that followed I was frequently overcome with emotion, overcome in ways that I hadn't been since the very first months after Paul's death. I was perhaps more overwhelmed with the sadness of his leaving me than I had ever been in those past sixteen months. I could be walking down the street, sitting in church or—very often—driving in my car, and my face would be instantly wet with tears.

Maybe it was the stone, and what it meant for me, but there was one other thing that happened, an odd collision of circumstances for which I had no explanation. My parents were visiting, renting a cottage on the lake near my house. One afternoon I went in to use the bathroom off their bedroom. I saw my father's pajamas hanging from the hook on the back of the door. He is a frugal man. I thought I recognized those pajamas from when I was growing up. It's possible. They were threadbare. I thought of Paul's pajamas, a nearly new pair, sitting in his drawer. I had given away some of his clothes, but the underwear and the pajamas I hadn't known what to do with. I went out and asked my father if he would like that new pair of pajamas. He seemed touched and said he thought it was a fine idea, so when I went home I pulled them out of the drawer. I held up the top. There was a watery pink stain across the neckline. I looked closer. I couldn't believe what I was looking at. I remembered at once that as Paul died, after the final breaths, Genevieve had taken a towel and gently placed it around his neck to absorb what flowed from his open mouth. Here was the stain from that moment. Those pajamas had somehow been put away in this drawer and only now was I discovering them, unwashed, unfolded. Did I know they were in there, and forget? Perhaps they had been washed and the stain never came out? Did I not want to wash them? This was, after all, a part of Paul, something that had come from him and, bizarre as it was, it was something to hold on to. I took them downstairs and put them in the washing machine. How could it be I was only doing this now? It was like a leftover chore, the last on my list of things to do. When the cycle spun dry, I pulled out the pajama top and held it up: the blue-and-white stripes were clean and new-looking, the stain gone. I hung them on the line in the sun and when they were dry I folded them and took them to my father.

This triggered more. Sudden, intense, very sensory memories arose, the sounds and smells and most of all the sights of the final days of Paul's illness. The sight of him, toward the end, that is what I remembered with the greatest resistance. The night after I gave those pajamas to my father, I got into bed and suddenly I could see Paul—not like a ghost, but the too-vivid memory of the back of his head on the pillow beside me, his neck swollen from the steroids he was taking to prevent the brain tumors from swelling, the puckering of his skin, the dryness of his scalp and the light downy wisps of hair coming out from under his hat. All this, the sight of the back of his neck, the oily feel of his skin, the swollen helpless look in his eyes, the way his wool hat slid to the side of his head, all this came rushing at me and the tears just came, unstoppable. Why now? I kept asking myself.

The following weekend I went to a party. I had been to many of these parties at the lake over the summer, with friends who are mostly single and somewhat younger than I. I enjoyed the wonderful feeling of freedom that came over me as I danced, using the music as a kind of magic-carpet ride away from the never-ending waves of grief and abandonment. But somehow, that night, I didn't feel like dancing. I sat in a chair at the edge of the room and watched my friends lapse into the rhythm of the evening. Their faces were at ease, almost blissful, as they moved around in the candlelight. I looked at them and I thought, you have your whole lives in front of you—there will be love and marriage and children and homes and dogs and grandchildren and lots and lots of fun parties like these. I wasn't exactly envious, though I suppose there was some of that. I was just reflecting, almost in awe, about what lies ahead of us at a certain age. My life was not over, I knew, yet much of those anticipations were over for me. There would be no children. I had had my one great love, and it was over. I couldn't seem to grasp what it was I could be heading for.

A couple of weeks after that Casimer called to tell me the stone was finished. I was excited, yet I searched my mind to see what else we could talk over. Wasn't there another detail to be discussed? Wasn't there just one thing left unfinished? It seemed not.

I had talked with my cousin George about coming

with me to get the stone and he hadn't hesitated. It certainly was something he wanted to do, he said. He lives two hours in the opposite direction, so we found a day that suited our schedules and planned to meet in Nashua and then drive together to Woods Hole for the ferry. We could only spare one day, so I made reservations on the nine o'clock ferry, returning at five. It's a three-hour drive from my house to Woods Hole, in my own car. The truck is slower, much slower. And there is Boston rush-hour traffic in between all that. So when the day came, I set the alarm for 4:00 A.M., to be on the safe side.

It was a dark, cool morning when I went out to start the truck. The stars were bright in their places and the air was still: a good chance we'd have a good day. The night before I had put several blankets and a moving quilt into the back, to cushion the stone in case of stormy seas. As a last thought, I added some rope and the tie-down from the boat trailer. I sat in the driveway, letting the engine warm for a few minutes. My neighbor's lights were not on, so the darkness was complete. The day before, around sunset, Dune and I walked to the grave. I sat beside the small wooden marker and I told Paul he was finally going to have a stone, one good enough for him. I told him I was going to get the stone in his truck, that I was going over on the ferry to the island. I told him I hoped he'd be with me. Sitting there in the dark truck, the heater gradually warming the cab, I said to Paul, okay, Bear, here we go, pulled on the headlights and set out.

I rarely take the truck any farther than to the store or to the dump, so I had checked the oil the day before and filled the tank with gas. I didn't know what else to check. Though it's nearly ten years old, there was no reason to think that the truck wasn't up to a trip like this. Paul cared for it with precision and I've tried to imitate his ways. Especially under the circumstances, I somehow felt there was no question that it would make it. As we rolled along from back roads to main roads to major highways, it moved with energy. I was feeling good, very good. In Nashua, George was waiting in the Friendly's parking lot and he seemed perhaps even more excited than I. George had brought his own box of rigging and tie-downs, blankets and foam cushioning.

The sun was just coming up, a pink and gold beginning, as we set out down the highway. George and I have always liked traveling together. We hitchhiked across the country one summer when we were still in college and ever since then, any chance for a trip together, however small, seems exciting. This of course was special, not so much a trip as a gesture, a ceremony we would act out together, a silent prayer in memory of a man we both missed very much.

We were the first truck into the hold. The vast empty space inside the big boat echoed with the sounds of engines as tractor trailers and delivery vans squeezed in around us. George and I put on the extra sweaters we'd brought and made our way to the upper deck.

I missed Paul so much just then. Though it hadn't occurred to me before that moment, it seemed so right to be bringing his stone home on a boat. Oddly, since we lived more in the woods than anywhere else, it seemed that we were always taking ferries. Paul had never been on a ferry before we met, but by the end of his life he'd been on quite a number of them. We hadn't planned that wedding trip on the island off the coast of Maine. We were driving along, north of Camden, on a beautiful October day just like this one, and we saw a sign for Islesboro, with an arrow.

"Islesboro," he said, "want to try it?"

We followed the arrow, which led to a ferry landing. "Oh," I said, "it's an island."

"Great," he said, "let's go." So we crossed over on a flat white ten-car ferry called *Governor Edmund Muskie*. The ferry to Block Island was another one we took several times, and once we rode the ferry across the Connecticut River, simply because the ferry, which was really a tugboat pushing a small barge, was so cute. It was a four-minute ride. We went over, Paul and I leaning against each other and the railing, looking down at the muddy river currents. When we reached the landing, a crescent worn into the hard dirt of the riverbank, we paid another fifty cents and returned.

The one we loved the most, though, was the ferry to Newfoundland. I had to go there on assignment, and Paul came along for fun. To get there, we had to take the ferry to Nova Scotia, which was a nine-hour ride from Portland to Yarmouth on a huge boat called *The Bluenose*. It had seven decks, a gambling casino and loud music in the bar. It was a long ride for two people who didn't much like to drink and who never gambled. But the ride to Newfoundland was on a retired icebreaker. The hull was battered and rust-streaked. And when we drove the car into the hold, brawny men took chains and blocks and tied it down with authority, a poor omen for the eleven-hour trip that lay ahead of us across the North Atlantic. We later read in one of Farley Mowat's books about a bulldozer on board a ferry on this same route. The 'dozer was tossed about so violently that it broke through the side of the boat and plunged into the sea, leaving a dozer-sized hole. Paul found that passage as he was reading in bed one night not long after our return, and he read it to me out loud and we laughed and laughed, remembering our own experience. On board that boat, which left port on a gray and windy afternoon, I fell seasick almost immediately and found a corner of a couch in the lounge and lay down to ride it out. Eventually every one of the rest of the dozen or so passengers found room on these couches and we lay like victims of some sudden plague, groaning together in our misery. Paul roamed about the boat placidly—and alone—as it lunged and bucked atop the cresting seas. At one point he knelt beside me, stroked my forehead and said, "I ordered you a hot turkey sandwich, Bear. I think it'll make you feel better." He had never been seasick, in fact had never encountered it before. His experience with boats was limited to our rowboat and the ferries we'd taken. He had no way of knowing what the mere mention of food can be like for someone under its spell.

"Did you order one for yourself?" I asked. My words were shameless groans.

"Yup," he said.

"Well, then," I said. "I think you ordered yourself two."

And he went back to the galley and ate the two platters and talked with the crew as the boat leapt and swayed its way to a midnight landing on the wild island of Newfoundland.

It was as different a landing as could be that day, as we moved steadily into the Vineyard, gently knocking against the pilings and coming to rest. If my recent trips to Oak Bluffs were any indication, it would seem that the town was always bathed in a glorious warm summer light, the colorful gingerbread houses lit like the skyline of a fairyland against a blue-sky backdrop. Within minutes we were parked in front of Casimer's little yellow studio. He came to the screen door and raised his hand in greeting. He was wearing a woolen cap and a heavy apron over a red flannel shirt. "I've got it all crated," he said, "but I left the top off so you could see it."

It was dark and cold inside. The stone was upright against the wall, tight inside a pine crate. The surface of the stone was a deep red, the color of brownstone. George knelt down beside it and ran his hand across it, smooth as glass. The trees Casimer had carved stood like soldiers behind the little house and enveloped it with the fullness of their leaves, just as it truly was. Once again I was overcome.

Casimer had made an elaborate diagram, like an architect's, of how the stone should be set in the ground and he discussed this with us, carefully outlining each step. We went over his instructions twice and I jotted extra notes in the margin of his drawing.

At last I told him how pleased I was with the stone. I couldn't really express it. I gave him the check I had made out before I left.

"We're all square?" I asked.

"Yes," he said and he began to finish packing the stone.

I was uncomfortably cold, my hands like ice. At last I stepped out the door and stood with the warm sun on my back, watching through the screen.

Casimer took cardboard and drawing paper and laid it against the face of the stone. He had cut loose pine boards to fit the top of the crate, and he began to nail it shut.

It took the three of us, using rollers and prybars and wedges and all our strength, to get it into the back of the truck. George used a tie-down to secure it.

When he was done, I looked inside. The stone looked small and slight. You could glance in, and if you didn't look carefully, you'd think the truck was empty.

We said good-bye to Casimer. He said he'd be waiting to hear from me, about the article I might write, and I said I'd be in touch. He stood on the cement step outside his shop and waved us off.

The ride back across the water was as smooth as it had been that morning. The sun was low on the horizon and sent beacons of orange light up into the clouds. George and I sat outside, on the upper deck, shivering inside our sweaters but always happy to be out in the salt air. We shared an apple and said little. I envisioned Paul's red truck in the hold beneath us, moving steadily, along with us, toward home.

"Paul would have loved this," I said, "the whole day, everything about it . . ." I didn't complete the thought. It seemed almost silly, and yet so real. I could see the smile of pleasure all of this would have brought to Paul's face.

"Yes," George said and when I turned to look at him, his eyes, like mine, were moist with tears.

After I left George off in Nashua, I drove the rest of the way home alone. It was very late. The dashboard lights cast a weak glow inside the cab. The truck rolled steadily along, the engine making the rhythmic whirring noises so peculiar to it, a sound I once held synonymous with Paul. Without George, I was suddenly very conscious of the stone in the back of the truck, a heavy, almost vocal presence. It was well past midnight when I pulled into our driveway. I got out and stood next to the truck. The stars overhead were as bright as they had been that morning. There was no moon. I said a small prayer of thanks for the safe delivery of the stone and went inside to bed.

Over the next couple of weeks, we set the stone. I had help. Mike. Ron. Mel. Jack. Those who, over those first two years, had done the jobs that Paul would have done. Mike (Genevieve's husband) made a set of back steps and he put a lock on the cellar door. Over the summer, Jack painted the house, inside and out. Ron finished the clapboards Paul had started at the barn. Mel helped me bring in the wood over the course of several crisp fall days.

We took shovels and a pickax from the shed and went up to the cemetery. It was surprising that there had not yet been a frost. The flowers were still pretty and bright. We dug them up and pulled up the wooden marker. The ground there is dense, clayey, and the digging was difficult.

Mike and Mel dug the hole. I was astonished that when the shovels hit against the cement casing of the coffin it didn't upset me. "Good," Mike said, "we can use this as a form for the cement." And we did. When it cured, we pried the pine boards off the top of the crate. It took three of us, grunting, to lift the stone out of the box and set it upright, steadying it with props. We put levels on the side and on the top and against the front, gently nudging the stone until all the bubbles lined up. Mike set his compass on the top. It pointed nearly due south. We filled in around the stone with loam we brought up in the truck, and planted it with pachysandra my father had sent from his garden. At last, we planted a yellow and red chrysanthemum on either side.

I planned a small service of dedication. I called the family—Paul's parents and his sisters, my aunt and uncle, George—and a few friends, and I asked Dick to be there. It seemed necessary, the last possible ceremony there could be in memory of Paul. I set it for a Sunday afternoon in October, the day after what would have been our sixth wedding anniversary. I knew I was doing this mostly for myself, a final joining of the forces that had kept me together since Paul's passing.

A few days before the service, I walked up to the grave with a small bucket of water and a cloth. In our digging and planting we had splattered the stone with flecks and smears of dirt and I wanted to wash it down. The earth was dry. I sat down beside the stone. Dune raced off toward the stone wall in pursuit of a chipmunk. The trees around the cemetery had turned, and in the late afternoon sun their branches sent out flares of reds and yellows and oranges.

I had dreamt the night before that I was on a bridge, a fine old arched bridge, crossing to the other side. I was on foot. There was some sense of urgency, some sense of danger. I had reached the middle of the bridge. A wide, swollen river rushed under me. Beyond was a cloud of thick white fog. I was standing still, hesitant to move on, when I woke up.

I knew that the dream was about my life. I needed to cross over now. What was behind me could not be reclaimed, and yet the prospect of what lay ahead was frightening and obscured. I was weary of grieving, weary of the sadness that kept crowding into my life no matter how much I pushed back against it. I was not weary of the memory of Paul, but I was tired of the sadness his passing had brought into my life. Above all, I was tired of being brave.

An image came up, sharp, of Paul sitting on our porch in the early spring warmth, a few weeks before he died. He liked sitting out there when he could. He was wearing two flannel shirts and the brown wool hat. He was somewhat hunched in his chair, the oxygen tube trailing in through the kitchen door where it connected with the machine. His breathing was loud and rough. I remember coming out that day to sit with him. A rhododendron we had transplanted from Bide-a-wee the previous fall was near the porch screen and we had been watching it anxiously. Though most everything around us had turned green and begun to blossom, the rhododendron appeared to have died over the winter. The leaves were brown and curled tight, like little cigars. That day, he raised his arm, with some effort, and pointed at it. "Look, Bear," he said. The plastic bridle of the oxygen tubes that hung over his ears and fed to his nose always made him look sad, but he was smiling weakly. I followed his finger. The plant was brown and withered. A goner. But then I saw it, too. A big white blossom coming up out of the center, a triumph of faith.

Right then, sitting beside the new stone, I wanted to be that flower. It seemed impossible, but then so had that bloom. So had Paul's life. I got on my knees and dunked the cloth in the bucket of water. I passed it over the smooth stone, tracing the letters as I rubbed. The slate washed down like a blackboard and the sun, hot against it, sucked the dampness off it almost as fast as I wet it. I went over it carefully, three or four times, down to the line that met the earth, where Casimer had signed his name, like any artist, and carved the date, 1990.

I stood up and backed off a few paces. The stone was

right. It said all that could be said in that small space about the man that I loved.

PAUL DOUGLAS BOLTON
DECEMBER 20, 1949-MAY 30, 1989
MASTER CARPENTER
GENTLE MAN
GRACEFUL SOUL
WE MISS YOU

I bent and kissed the stone, called to Dune and walked back home.

About the Author

EDIE CLARK has been writing and editing from her home in New Hampshire for the past twenty years. She has written extensively about New England in feature stories for *Yankee* magazine, where she has served as senior editor, senior writer and fiction editor. Her multiple-part series on land development, water pollution, the Christian Science church and the Connecticut River have gained widespread attention. When she isn't writing, she is gardening, or working on her old house.